KIDS WHO KILL

from Deafness into Darkness

Based on true stories

PHYLLIS K. WALTERS

KIDS WHO KILL

FROM DEAFNESS INTO DARKNESS

PHYLLIS K. WALTERS

------- Since 2016 -------
AHA! PRESS
A Howard Activity, LLC

Edited by Paula F. Howard, Aha! Press, an imprint of A Howard Activity, LLC

Cover Design by Robert Hurley, Best Impressions Book Design

ISBN: 979-8-9860707-9-7

PRINTED IN THE UNITED STATES OF AMERICA

Dedication

I would like to dedicate this book to my sister-in-law, Janet Walters Chandler (6/1/1943 - 5/1/2023), whose encouragement and support strengthened me in my moments of doubt and weakness. She has been a warrior through her own battles yet has taken the time and energy to pray for me and serve as a beacon of hope.

CONTENTS

CHAPTER ONE

A SOLITARY FIGURE sat at a square table in the waiting area of the Lucas County Juvenile Detention Center. Shifting in his seat, he looked over to a single door at the end of the room. No one had entered yet.

Here I am waiting for a corrections officer to bring my son, Noah, to see me. It's almost Christmas, how sad this year. Noah will be wearing an orange jumpsuit and flip-flops. He'll be wearing ankle chains and handcuffs to restrain his movements all because he happened to be in the wrong place at the wrong time. Not the way I want to see my son.

I can't believe he's capable of murder. There's got to be more to his story.

Lost in thought, Noah's father began remembering the past: How he and his wife had prayed to have a son. *We visited fertility specialists and had genetic counseling to be sure we weren't carrying any genes for a child with severe birth defects.*

Then God blessed us with a son. He was perfect. Almost. He just couldn't hear. He was born with a congenital hearing problem.

The doctors said it could have been due to an infection my wife suffered during pregnancy, maybe the rubella virus.

Around her third month of pregnancy, I remember her visiting a friend whose little girl had German measles. We didn't think much of it, nor about how sick she felt a few days later. but the doctors thought that might have caused our own son's deafness. Imagine, something as small as that, yet it has affected our Noah his entire life.

Again, the man looked around at others in the room, talking in small groups of two or three, then at the doorway. Still no one.

It'll be nice for them to take his handcuffs off so he can use sign language with me, like usual, It's just the ankle cuffs that'll have to stay on, he thought.

People who used certified American Sign Language (ASL) were always available for Noah's visitors and interpreted his words, like for Dr. Rosie Klein, a court appointed psychologist who would make sure Noah understood the charges against him.

...and, of course, his useless public defender, the man thought. *I like Dr. Klein. The public defender asked for her to be appointed. But that's the only good thing he's done for Noah.*

Looking up again, he expected the door to open at any moment.

Do I have regrets? Yeah, I have my share and I know Noah's mother must have more than a few. First off, I regret placing him in a boarding school for the deaf at the tender age of just five years old. I justified that decision because after his mother and I split, I commuted ninety minutes each way to work and taught classes on Saturday twice a month. Having him in boarding school just seemed the best way to provide twenty-four-hour care for him.

After a few years there, how could I know Noah would be

abused by other residents and staff? How could I possibly have suspected that would happen? Or that at thirteen, he would be susceptible to peer pressure and get into serious trouble?

Why didn't I just change careers after his mother left me? With all my education, I thought being a tenured college professor was the best way to provide for him financially. But with hindsight, it's easy to realize how much my ego and pride influenced my decision-making.

Once his mother ran off with 'the milkman,' so to speak, I had no partner to help me with alternative solutions for our son. But I know that's no excuse for failing him.

His mother will be visiting him later today. I just hope I'm gone by then. I can barely stand looking at her. I'm glad that jerk she left us for left her for a younger model. It serves her right.

A noise at the door announced the arrival of the guard and Noah Campbell as they entered. Mr. Campbell looked up at the boy he loved and watched him walk over.

"Hi Dad," the young boy signed with his lips and fingers. His dad stood and hugged him tightly. Noah's balance was somewhat impaired by the restraints on his ankles.

"Hello son," Mr. Campbell his father signed. "Would you like something to eat or drink? I've got a debit card I can use at the vending machine. The guard said you can't be by the snacks, but I can get whatever you want. Oh, and just so you know, the coffee machine is broken."

"I'll take a soda and a peanut candy bar, if you have enough money on the card," Noah signed.

Mr. Campbell walked to the machines, inserted his card, and bought two sodas, the candy, and a package of gum. He also thought about what to say to Noah.

Should I bring up the murder charge against him or just ask how he likes his new lawyer?

Returning to the table, Mr. Campbell popped open the two cans, and slid the candy across to his son. Then he put the package of gum and can tabs into his shirt pocket. Noah wasn't allowed to have metal on him.

"How do you like your new attorney, Dan Singer," he asked his son.

The young boy nodded his head. "He seems interested in me. I think he'll do a good job. I'm not just a 'number' to him like that public defender guy made me feel," Noah signed, his fingers flew as the words poured out while his dad watched. "Mr. Singer said he'd be back in a couple of days. He told me that a lady doctor would be coming to talk to me to make sure I understand what's happening."

"He told me the same thing," Mr. Campbell signed. "Be sure to tell him all the details so he can represent you right. Oh, and be very honest with the psychologist. She'll ask about your childhood."

Campbell knew that Noah used sign language when he was nervous and read lips when he was comfortable. Right now, Noah looked a little nervous. "It's okay, son, if we continue to sign, nobody will know what we're saying, right?" Mr. Campbell winked at his son.

Noah looked around the room and nodded. No one was paying any attention to them. The novelty of seeing a deaf person signing with visitors had obviously worn off.

"I didn't mean to hurt that lady, Dad, but she came at me with a knife out of nowhere! I just grabbed the gun from my pocket and shot her. Honest, it was self-defense!" Tears moistened his eyes as his father looked at him.

Campbell reached across the table and patted the top of Noah's hands, both palms were down on the table in front of him. Noah's head hung low and Mr. Campbell ruffled his son's hair.

What was he doing with a gun? he wondered, but didn't want to press the issue at this time.

"I'm off from school until mid-January, so I'll drive up to Toledo and visit again on Christmas Eve and Christmas Day. I already have a hotel room booked. Hope you don't mind pizza for dinner on Christmas Eve. Christmas Day, we can order whatever you like, but today is the last day I can put our order in."

"What are my choices?"

"You can have turkey with gravy, mashed potatoes, cranberry sauce, and green beans or ham, sweet potatoes, salad, and cherry pie."

"I'd like the turkey. But can I have the cherry pie, too?"

"I'm sure that can be worked out, Noah."

"Thanks, Dad. I'm lucky that Juvie lets parents visit on a holiday. I've heard that other places don't, even on Christmas."

"Maybe by next year we'll enjoy food and football at home. I'm selling the house in Walnut Hills and waiting to see where we can be living together. If you must serve time, I want to live close by. Then, after spring quarter, I'll be retiring."

"You aren't selling because of the cost of my defense, are you? I would hate that."

"Don't worry, it's not that. Really, it's the yard . . . too much work anymore."

———

When the guard said I had a visitor, I knew it was my dad, Noah remembered later when he was back in his room. *I was ashamed for him to see me in this orange jumpsuit with handcuffs and ankle restraints. But I suppose all visits will be like that. He didn't seem distant at all today. He even hugged me. With my handcuffs off, I reached out and hugged him back but almost fell into him with my ankles shackled together. I could hardly hold back my tears. I felt ashamed.*

Noah turned over on his bed and stared at the ceiling. Then he reached for his journal and began writing his thoughts.

When my trial comes, all I can hope is that they try me as a juvenile. I've never been to the 'big joint,' but from what people have told me, it 'ain't pretty.'

My new attorney is really cool, but brutally honest, too. He hasn't given me much hope for seeing the light of day outside the prison exercise area where we get about an hour a day.

Mr. Singer said he plans to enter a 'not guilty' plea on the charge of murder against me. He just wants me to admit to kidnapping the little boy. I'm glad my dad got me an experienced lawyer. Even if he has little hope for a self-defense motive. 'When you burglarize a home, the owner has the right to self-defend with a weapon,' he told me. I didn't know that. But how was I supposed to know that lady was in the kitchen? I didn't expect anybody to be home.

I used to think my dad was a big jerk . . . 'a big wig professor.' Now, I understand he was only doing what he thought was in my best interest. He figured I would get the best daily care and education at the boarding school. But what they told him and what I received were two different things. I got an education . . . that's for sure . . . just not the kind any parent would expect.

When I was about five, I read my dad's lips when he told my first psychologist, Dr Erickson, that Mom felt guilty. He made excuses for her and even blamed himself. He told Dr. Erickson that Mom didn't realize I couldn't hear. 'Developmentally delayed, without age-appropriate speech.' That's how I was labeled at two years old. Still no diagnosis of deafness until I was four. Instead of finding ways and people to help me, Mom ran away.

I will never forget my first session with Dr. Erickson. She was really a nice lady, kind and gentle. I liked that. After my dad left the room, we played a board game called Parcheesi. It didn't take words to explain it and I caught on right away. But once my dad put me in St. Rita's, I never saw Dr. Erickson again.

My next counselor, Dr. Adler, was assigned by a priest at St. Rita's. That came after I bit an older kid for taking my cupcake on my seventh birthday! Dr. Adler told me my anger was 'misdirected.' I hate to admit it, but I was angry at both of my parents for pushing me away.

Adler pointed out that it was my mother who abandoned me. He said I shouldn't be taking it out on the other kids or any authority figures. And he warned me to never do it to girls or women.

Then last Christmas, without notice, 'mother, dear' waltzed back into the picture, acting like a loving, concerned mom. But I remember her smacking me in the face for not listening when Dad was at work. I think she was unhappy, herself. But why did she have to spank me with the wooden spoon and put me in the dark closet for what she called 'time-out.' Whose 'time-out,' Mom? Yours? She said she was sorry, but I couldn't hear her. She didn't realize I couldn't hear anything.

Yeah, and she's supposed to be coming here today. Do I really care?

My dad said he'll be back, again, soon. He's trying to work things out with my lawyer. I'm starting to trust him, again. My dad is keeping his word. And I'm proud of him for learning sign language, and never giving up on me. I deserve it if he does. What a screw-up I've been.

Well, enough journaling. I'm glad my friend, Randy Evans, gave me this book when I left Indian River Juvenile Center. He said writing my thoughts would help. I think it does.

CHAPTER TWO

"YOU'RE MISTAKEN OFFICER. I *have* been approved for visitation with my son, Noah Campbell," the woman said in an exasperated tone. Melody Campbell-Russell stood with her arms crossed in front of her chest and peered over her glasses at the sergeant seated behind the glass partition.

"I will check the list again, Mrs. Russell," Sergeant Monahan said in a firm, professional voice.

"I specifically requested a 1:30 appointment because my flight wasn't arriving in Detroit until 11:00 a.m. And my name is *not* Mrs. *Russell.* The name is *hyphenated* as in Campbell-Russell; and secondly, I go by *Doctor*."

"My apologies, *Doctor* Campbell-Russell. You'll be glad to know that I *did* find your name under "C" for Campbell-Russell. May I see your identification?" The sergeant waited before directing her to sign in the logbook. "I'll call to have your son brought down."

He picked up the phone and hit a button. "This is Monahan. Bring inmate Noah Campbell down to visitation." Then he looked at the woman again. "Doctor, place your purse in the bin and step through the metal detector. I'll direct you to the secure visitation area. Your driver's license will be returned when you sign out." He handed her a badge with "visitor" in capital letters.

"Fine. Thank you."

Melody turned in her driver's license, put her purse in the bin, and secured her visitor's badge to the lapel of her navy-blue suit jacket. She waited for the buzzer, then walked through the door as instructed by Monahan. The small, narrow hall felt as if it were closing in on her and the sixty seconds between buzzers at each end of the hall felt like an eternity. She noticed the security camera above her. The second door buzzed. She opened the door and entered a large, windowless room with six-foot tables and folding chairs. An officer directed her to a nearby table. Rather than sit, she stood, waiting for her son to arrive.

Not very private, she thought. *This is the first time I've seen Noah since last Christmas. I guess we can hug, if it's allowed and if he is open to one. The other visitors are having pizza and drinks. Wonder how they got it . . . maybe they ordered it in advance. Next time I'll know. That is, if there is a next time. Who knows what the visitation guidelines will be at his next facility.*

She continued waiting while thinking: *What a difference a year makes. How could he have gotten into such a mess? He had such a great future. The Ohio School for The Deaf (OSFD) would have housed him until his twenty-first birthday and provided much needed vocational training to ensure a productive, adult life. Or even better, they said he is very bright. He might have gone to Gallaudet University in D.C. It is an exceptional university for the deaf. Heaven knows his father and I could have afforded the tuition.*

I doubt he would qualify for financial aid with two parents making six figures.

Noah tapped his mother on the shoulder. She hadn't seen him enter the room but now turned around to see his wrists in handcuffs while he signed, "Hello Mother." The correction officer released the cuffs, turned, and walked to the doorway where he stood for the duration of their visit.

"Why, Noah, you look as if you have lost a few pounds and grown a couple inches," Melody said with a smile. Noah had already sat in one of the chairs and gestured for her to sit across from him. He placed his hands in his lap, out of reach.

Melody knew that Noah read lips as she did. So, she hadn't requested an interpreter for the visit. For one thing, it would have created even less privacy than they already had with the guard standing nearby. *Such a large visitation area,* she thought.

Even though the law states that an inmate is entitled to an ASL certified interpreter, if requested by either party, Noah had agreed that it wasn't necessary. Besides, he wasn't sure how long he could tolerate a visit from his mother or if she would tolerate what he had to say. He had found her conversation inappropriate the last time he saw her but had kept his thoughts to himself. But this time, he needed answers.

"A lot has changed in a year, for both of us, right, Mother?" From his facial expression, she could see that his comment and question had hidden meaning.

"Mother, I want to ask you something." He said, not waiting for an acknowledgement. "Why did you leave? Why haven't you written or remembered my birthdays?"

"I don't know if your dad told you, Noah, but I am divorced now and living in Portugal."

"Divorced, again? What name will you claim *this* time?"

He shook his head and looked away.

Instead of answering, she changed the subject by asking, "Have you met your new attorney?"

"I did, and to answer your next question, I like him very much. Don't evade my last question, Mother. What's your name now, please? and my next question: Why Portugal?"

Ordinarily Melody's response to that last question would be "why not?" Under these circumstances, she viewed her son's interest as worthy of reasonable responses.

She faced her son and tried to answer. "Well, Noah, my choice of partners has brought nothing but hardship and pain. After leaving your father, I completed my master's degree and married my professor, as you may know. He was not 'the milkman' as your father likes to describe him. However, he did turn out to be a philanderer who couldn't keep his pants zipped when it came to doting, attractive, undergraduate students.

"Then I met Mr. Right. But, once again, I was wrong. That one was into pornography. After I couldn't get him to stop, I found photos and correspondence with underage girls. That's when I left."

Noah showed no emotion but simply looked at his mother. "Do you believe in God?"

Melody was taken aback by his response. With tears forming in her eyes, she said, "Yes, of course, or I wouldn't have born *you*. We prayed to have you; you know." She took a tissue from her purse and blotted her wet cheeks, then looked down. She couldn't face looking at her son. She felt his question was meant to crucify her for leaving him in the first place. "I must admit that I was angry with God for bringing my precious boy into the world without the ability to hear."

"Did it ever occur to you how angry *I* would be that you

left me?" Noah was signing rapidly now. "Did you think about *any*one else at all? Or did the inconvenience of raising a special needs kid overwhelm you? You didn't cope well, did you? Your discipline was sneaky and harsh. How could you take your wedding vows so lightly? How can you say you love me?"

"I know that 'sorry' isn't good enough for the damage I've created, Noah. All I have to offer is my apology and my promise to always be available to you for whatever you need now or in the future."

"Okay, Mother, for starters, do you think living in Portugal is going to let you keep your promise? It's not like you can spend a lot of quality time with me. And my needs can't be met by money, Mother. Are you living there for work or with some guy for pleasure? Beautiful environment, right? Look at mine!" He swept his arm around the room. "Only *mine* will be getting worse very soon."

Noah stood and clenched his fists. The officer at the door took a step forward. Noah abruptly sat back down and took a deep breath. *No, I'm not leaving until I get some answers.*

Melody was so startled by her son's response that she could only look down. Then she looked up at her young son. "I've completed my Ph.D. in Psychology at Central Florida University and have been accepted into a three-year post-doc internship in Lisbon, Portugal. I will be teaching English and Psychology to undergrad students to prepare them for international careers. I plan to visit you on school breaks throughout the year." She could tell he was reading her lips closely. But then, he looked away.

He quietly rose from his chair, turned his back, and walked toward the guard. Melody watched his back as his foot restraints hindered his steps. She sat there and wept.

CHAPTER THREE

"Hi boss, I have an important message for you," said Ruthie with a smile. Dr. Rosie Klein placed her worn, brown leather, briefcase on a chair in the entry way and took the note from Ruthie's hand.

"Oh, Dan Singer. I wonder what that charming attorney wants today?" Rosie said. She remembered him well. He had asked her to evaluate his client, Angel Morgan, who had been charged with murder along with three other co-defendants in a multiple murder trial a while ago..

"I'll call him before I get started with my nine-o'clock appointment. Did it sound urgent?"

"He asked if I could mark it 'ASAP' on the message," Ruthie said. "But they all expect that, right?"

"Would you mind bringing me a mug of coffee? I'll give him a call. By the way, your smile starts my mornings with joy and gratefulness, Ruthie."

"Sure thing on the coffee, and ditto on *your* smile."

Rosie sat in her comfortable wingback chair and made the

call. “Good morning, this is Dr. Rosie Klein. Attorney Singer is expecting my call. Is he available?”

“As a matter of fact, he is,” the receptionist said. “A message stuck to my phone says to ‘put Dr. Klein’s call through no matter what.’” Rosie recognized the woman’s sweet voice.

“Hi, Becky Joy. Any more charity golf outings? We had fun last time, didn’t we?”

“We sure did, Rosie.”

She heard the phone click and a male’s voice greeted her. “Hi, Rosie. . . good to hear your voice. I have another case for you if you’re available.” Without waiting for her reply, Singer continued. “The public defender was about to have you appointed just before the client’s father fired him and retained me. I thought that was a good move, so I’ve decided to call you myself. I saw the kid for the first time recently. He’s a deaf juvenile who stole a car from a shopping center parking lot in Worthington. He found the owner’s address in the glove compartment and drove to the woman’s house in West Toledo where he robbed her, shot her, and abducted her four-year-old.”

“Oh, my. Sounds like a horrible story,” Rosie said. “What’s the victim’s name?”

“Misty Matthews,” Singer said.

“Well, the University of Toledo classes that I teach are on holiday break until later in January,” Rosie said, “so I can make the time.”

“Great,” Singer said. “Glad to hear it. I’ll get the discovery materials to you right away so you can review them.”

“What’s this young man’s name and where is he housed?” Rosie asked while grabbing a legal pad and felt tip pen.

“His name is Noah Campbell, age sixteen. He’s being held

in the Lucas County Juvenile Detention Center for the time being. You know where it's located, right? I will let the corrections officers know to add your name to the professional visitation list. I'll also contact the prosecutor, Brooks Wright, and have Judge Dee Warner appoint you. Noah is deaf and the issue is competency. There will be two certified ASL interpreters in the sessions with you. You know that's the law, right? I will forward the discovery packet to your downtown office this afternoon."

"Sounds like a plan, Dan," she chuckled at the rhyme. "By the way, why was the woman shopping so far from her home in Toledo?"

"The story goes that she and her son were visiting her sister and nephew. There are videos of them in the children's section of a shopping mall bookstore, having lunch at a food court, and walking into the parking garage. When they couldn't find her car, they called security and security called the local police. I've spoken to the victim's sister, Nora Douglas. She's confirmed that they returned to her house before she drove them back to Toledo."

"I'll need contact numbers for all the significant people in Noah's life and I'll call Brooks Wright after you let him know I'm on the case. As I recall, he was the prosecutor on the Randy Evans case. What's Noah's father's name?"

"It's Dr. Kirk Campbell. I'll get everything you've requested sent over to you, Rosie."

"Thanks Dan."

"Oh, thank *you,* Rosie. It's great to be working with you, again."

. . .

Rosie took a sip of steaming, hot coffee from her favorite ceramic mug, a gift from Bucky who had presented it to her in a small, square, black box covered with shredded, red tissue paper. Two sides of the mug had a verse from her favorite Robert Frost poem:

"Two roads diverged in a woods" was printed on one side and "I took the one less traveled by" was printed on the other.

Inside the mug, Bucky had placed a pouch containing a pair of red, octagon cut, drop earrings by Swarovski. She loved his gifts and was grateful he was the kind of husband who enjoyed giving her pretty things. For their weekly date nights, Rosie always wore the earrings as a reminder of her devotion to him.

She remembered that special evening in St. Martin at the quaint French restaurant where he had gifted her the mug after dessert, Cherries Jubilee. How fun it had been. Now, it reminded her to call him about making a reservation at their favorite restaurant for tonight.

After topping off her coffee, Rosie walked into the entry way to tell Ruth to hold her first client while she called Bucky. "Hey, Ruthie, if Ellie gets here, chat with her for a couple minutes, will you? I want to touch base with Bucky. I think she's selling girl scout cookies for her daughter. Please commit to three boxes and you can pick your favorites."

"Great ideas, Rosie. You calling Bucky and me ordering cookies are two ways to make my day. That's because if you don't call him, he will bug me to death, and if we don't get you eating cookies, you'll wither away to nothing." Ruth and Rosie laughed as Ellie, a stout middle-aged, attractive woman, came through the door.

Rosie hustled back to her office and made the call but it went to voicemail.

"You aren't answering, Bucky, dear," she recorded her message. "You must be in a department meeting. I'm calling to ask you to make reservations at Giovanni's tonight at 7:00. Ruth wants to fatten us up, so I figure Italian pasta will serve that purpose. Bye for now. See you at about 6:15. Oh, and do you mind taking Jocko for a walk around the block? That is, if you get home at your usual time at five?"

Ruth tapped gently on the door. "Ellie says we will get a discount if we buy six boxes. What do you think, boss lady?"

"That's fine. Bucky likes mint chocolate to go with our red wine in the evening. By the way, I'm ready to see Ellie. You can tell her to come on back now."

CHAPTER FOUR

THE BLACK DAY in Noah's life was a Friday. The day had started early when he picked up his journal. But it was around mid-afternoon, when he hit the crossroad that would determine the rest of his life.

Okay, I'm going to write this down. My therapist said journaling is like talking to someone, so I'll try it, since there's nobody else around.

How can I get through this winter with only my bike? It's so cold at 3:30 in the morning that riding two miles just to pick up papers for my route feels too long. Sometimes I can't even see when the wind or snow makes my eyes water. Customers complain if their papers are wet, then I have to pay for them. It all sucks.

Gray days just make the damp, cold weather even less bearable. At least today is sunny. I think I'll go for a walk in the warm shopping mall. If I had more money, I'd buy my dad and Ruby, my landlady, something for Christmas. Maybe even her sister, Rita.

• • •

Around noontime, now dressed in blue jeans and a red sweatshirt with black letters, Randy was just leaving the mall feeling somewhat disheartened. He knew his only option for Christmas gifts was going to be the dollar store. With a brisk wind blowing and temperatures dropping, he decided to cut through the adjacent parking garage. That's when he noticed a vehicle similar to the one his friend, the preacher's kid (PK), had once stolen.

He tried the driver's door and was surprised to find it unlocked. He looked around and saw no one, then jumped into the car, and remembered how to jumpstart the engine from watching his friend. The engine started. Noah drove slowly out of the garage trying not to draw any attention. He only planned to park it down the street from the boarding house just like he saw college students do every day.

But that isn't what actually happened.

"Been rather quiet this shift, Doug, hasn't it?" Detective Rachel Adams looked over at her partner, Detective Doug Ford.

"Unusually so. Let's go inside and get a pizza instead of eating in the car, again. I hate slopping it on our shirts, Rach, and watching you get it on your chin." Doug laughed.

A short time later, after having the owner wave the cost for them, Doug slid out of the booth to take a call from Dispatch outside.

Although the privately owned restaurant usually comped meals for cops and firefighters, Rachel left a generous tip on the table for their server. Through the window, she noticed Doug's subdued expression and watched him suddenly halt in his tracks. He beckoned to her over his shoulder as he picked up his pace and headed toward their unmarked vehicle.

She quickly followed and tossed the pizza box, still holding two pieces, onto the back seat, then put her diet Pepsi in the drink holder. Before she could secure her seat belt, Doug accelerated forward. *So much for a quiet shift,* she thought.

"A woman was murdered in her house on Lambert Lane in West Toledo; her four-year old son was located by an Ohio State Highway Patrolman at the Bowling Green rest area," Doug said. "Dispatch said the same woman reported her car stolen yesterday from a Worthington shopping center. It's pretty obvious the perp used her registration info to track her down at her house. For what purpose, we don't know."

"Were there any witnesses?" Rachel asked.

"Not likely. Dispatch said a Sgt. Ron Thompson, discovered her body when he took the boy home. The kid is smart. He knew his street address and told the officer. Said he didn't see or hear any shooting at his house but provided a clear description of his abductor. White, wearing blue jeans, a red sweatshirt with black letters and black tennis shoes. We don't know if he's the guy who shot the woman, only that he was party to a crime."

"Weird. Why would he grab a kid then release the little guy? He's obviously not a professional. Once the kid saw his face, a pro would never have allowed him to go free," Rachel said. Her thoughts went to her own children when they were that age.

"I'll talk to Thompson. You're good with kids, Rachel. If the boy is there, see if you can talk to him."

"Okay. Maybe his father or another family member will be there with him."

Doug parked in front of the house. The front door was open and uniformed policemen were walking in and out; everyone was busy with jobs investigating the location. An ambulance was in the driveway with two EMT's sliding a stretcher holding a black body bag into the back of the vehicle. Reporters and cameramen were standing around in small groups at the compelling scene. They slipped beneath the yellow crime scene tape and Rachel entered through the open door. Two local uniformed officers and a state highway patrolman were standing in the living room to the right of the hallway.

A despondent looking man was seated on a tan, leather love seat holding a small boy closely on his lap. No one was speaking. The boy clutched a plastic dinosaur to his chest. His father began to rub his back. When the three officers saw the detectives, they left the living room and led Rachel and Doug down the hall into the kitchen, sidestepping a pool of blood; all of them took out their paper note pads.

"I'm Detective Ford, and this is my partner, Detective Adams. What have you got so far?" Sgt. Thompson greeted them with a nod. "I got a call that there was a small boy approaching travelers and asking for a ride home. One woman wrapped a blanket around him and sat beside him on a bench until I arrived. I was approximately four miles away heading South toward the Findlay post. When I got there, the boy saw my uniform, jumped up, and asked me to take him home."

"I understand he's only four, how did you know where he lives?" Adams asked.

"He's a smart little guy and knew his street address, but

not his town. It was easy to go from there and pinpoint his house. No missing kid had been reported, but when we pulled into the driveway, he acknowledged it was his house. The lights were off in the residence and no car in the immediate vicinity, so I had him stay in my vehicle and called for back-up." Sgt. Thompson nodded toward small group. "Those officers are talking to the neighbor now."

"The next-door neighbor saw us pull up and walked over to my side of the cruiser. I rolled down the window and she introduced herself and asked if there was a problem. She recognized Scottie in the child's restraining seat and said she had noticed the house was dark which was unusual for that time of evening."

Thompson opened his notebook and read from it. "Her name is Phoebe Grant and her daughter, Amelia, attends the same pre-school as Scottie. She and the victim, Misty Matthews, carpool with another woman down the street. Scottie wanted out of the car so I released the straps and he immediately jumped into Mrs. Grant's arms. She offered to take him to her house for some food. He seemed comfortable with her, so I agreed, before entering the home of the victim."

Detective Adams was writing down his sequence of events, witness names, and numbers, including the woman at the rest area. Detective Ford was speaking with the local police officers who responded to the scene after being dispatched.

Adams returned to the living room and closed the door. Mr. Matthews turned to acknowledge her. "Mr. Matthews. I'm Detective Rachel Adams. I'm very sorry for your loss, sir. Could you come down to the precinct in the morning? I would like to ask you some questions."

"Sure, I'll do everything I can to help find the savage who

killed my wife," Mr. Matthews responded slowly with halting words and tears in his eyes. He took a deep breath and looked down at his son.

"Your neighbor next door is more than willing to help you with whatever you need."

"We're okay for now. Phoebe brought Scottie to me as soon as I pulled into the driveway. He and I need some time alone. I don't want to let him out of my sight, you understand. But I may ask her to watch him in the morning when I come talk to you."

Adams bent down and picked up the green, plastic dinosaur lying on the carpet in front of Scottie. She assumed it was the one Scottie had with him during his abduction and rescue. She placed it in the boy's lap and put her hand on top of one of his and patted it.

"Does your dinosaur have a name, Scottie?"

The boy clutched the dinosaur but did not look up. "Yes, ma'am. Her name is Misty. And I wuv her vewy, vewy much."

Scottie's response startled Scottie's father who could not hold back the tears. Knowing that Misty was his mother's name, Rachel figured Scottie had just changed the dinosaur's name on the spur of the moment and probably its gender, as well.

"How very nice, Scottie," Detective Adams said. "I hope to see you, again." She exited the living room and walked straight out the front door leaving her partner wondering what just happened.

"How did it go?" Doug asked.

Rachel was struggling with her emotions. "Give me a minute, Doug." She swallowed the lump in her throat and climbed in the passenger seat of their car. Her emotions were near the surface when minors were involved. "How did your interview go with Phoebe Grant?"

"Very informative as it pertains to the victim's life. They've been next door neighbors since both were pregnant with their kids. Good friends . . . husbands grilled out about once each weekend. Misty took good care of her kid and worked the graveyard shift stocking shelves at Walmart. Phoebe thought that was kind of risky, working through the night like that. Little did she think that a shopping trip in broad daylight would result in a car theft, let alone her friend's murder."

"So, was she saying that Misty slept during the day while Scottie was in school?"

"Yup. She'd probably gotten up, picked up her kid, and started dinner when the home invasion took place," Doug said.

"Terrible. You wonder if that little boy will ever adjust to life without his mother, don't you? Oh, and both Matthews and Scottie are spending the night with the Grants next door. Can't say I blame them. I wouldn't be able to sleep in the same house where someone I loved was murdered, either. Could you?"

CHAPTER FIVE

NOAH DROVE QUICKLY out of the rest area trying not to look back at the spot where he left the little boy. He had seen the fear and confusion on the boy's face and knew the vision of his mother lying on the floor at their house would haunt him for a long while.

It reminded him of the time his own father had dropped him off at St. Rita's and left him alone with Sister Marian. They had taken him to a dorm room, put his clothes away in a dresser and lined his shoes against one closet wall. He was allowed to keep a few personal things, a little blue blanket with satin edges, his stuffed orange and black Tiger, and the framed photo of himself with his dad. That picture meant everything to him. They were holding a large fish and had big grins on their faces.

Now, the loneliness engulfed him again as he watched the little boy growing smaller in his rearview mirror, standing alone, watching the car drive away.

I'll drive to my boarding house in Columbus, Noah thought, where he had stashed some things along with the victim's cell phone. *I wonder if it'll need a password? Maybe I can use it to call my dad.* As he drove, he observed the speed limits, not wanting to draw attention to himself in a stolen vehicle.

Arriving, he pulled behind the garage in the alley where Ruby and Rita parked their cars and quickly entered the cellar door in the back of the three-story house. It was the door he used to take out trash to the alley for pick-up.

His room was one floor up with a common-use bathroom down the hall. His stomach was upset and he reached the bathroom just in time before throwing up in the toilet. Slowly he washed his hands. Still undetected, he unlocked his boarding room door. Once inside, he tried the phone and found it was unlocked. He left a text for his dad with an urgent message to call him back, then set the phone on vibrate. He sat on his bed and waited. If his dad was teaching, he could expect a text back in about an hour.

He's probably teaching one of his fifty-minute classes that meets three days a week, Noah thought.

It was several hours later before Noah's father returned his son's text. He finally saw the conversation which had come across in block letters.

Dad, something's happened. It's bad. I don't know what to do, Noah had texted.

Knowing his son had run away from OSFD weeks before and was living somewhere in a Columbus boarding house, his father hadn't thought any laws had been broken. At first, Dr. Campbell had tried convincing Noah to return to Cincinnati and live with him. But Noah said he was going to make it on his own and would keep in touch. And now he had.

But Noah's next text was unbelievable as he admitted what had happened.

I didn't mean to hurt her Dad, it was self-defense. She had a knife!

Noah explained his version of the attack in his text, from her lunging at him with a kitchen knife, to catching him robbing her house. His fingers flew swiftly, spelling it all out. His deafness all the more frustrating now since he desperately wanted to be telling his dad the entire story in person.

You need to turn yourself in, Noah. Running just makes you look guilty, his father texted back. *I can call the highway patrol for you and explain that you just left the boy off near Bowling Green. Let them arrest you. If you don't, and they will come after you; they could shoot you.*

After considering everything, Noah planned to comply with his father's instructions and texted it back to him. Then, after they had finished, Noah looked out his bedroom window and couldn't believe what he saw. Officers in SWAT uniforms with helmets were surrounding the house and backyard.

How did they find me so quickly? He wondered as he texted his dad again: *Too late. Love you, Dad.*

He exited his room with his hands in the air and ran smack into two officers in the hall. They quickly searched him, removed the stolen jewelry from his pockets, cuffed him, called off their teammates, and led him out front to a waiting patrol car. He noticed the stolen car was already being towed by a police vehicle.

"Suspect has been apprehended without incident.

Bringing him in." Noah watched the lips of the patrol officer speaking into his microphone. He gestured to them that he couldn't hear but could lip-read. Then he wondered if his one and only phone call could be a text to his father.

CHAPTER SIX

CHAPLAIN TOM BECK slid into the long wooden pew beside a young dark-skinned man who seemed deep in thought. "Good morning, James," he said.

"Good morning, Sir." James replied, looking up and recognizing the man he admired. Extending his right hand. The chaplain shook it firmly and smiled back.

"I figured I'd find you here thirty minutes before our morning bible study. There's something I'd like to invite you to do. Would you accompany me to the Juvenile Facility in Toledo? I'm visiting a young deaf man there who will likely serve maximum time for shooting a woman whose house he burglarized. It's a long, complicated story that we can talk about on the way, if you want to go."

"I would like that. May I ask when and, why me, sir?"

"Well, this young man signs and reads lips. I've heard that you took American Sign Language in high school and I think he would appreciate communicating with you. Since you've been serving time here for the past thirteen years, I imagine you have lots of advice and encouragement to offer him. When he ages out of Juvenile, he'll be transferred here since he will likely be serving thirty to life."

"Where's he from and what's his name?"

"His name is Noah Campbell from Cincinnati, Ohio. He spent most of his sixteen years in boarding schools for deaf children."

"Why was he in boarding schools, is he an orphan? Does he have faith?"

"He's not an orphan. It's just that his father, a kind man, thought it was best for Noah to be in boarding school to get twenty-four-hour care because the home environment was . . . well, complicated. I've met him. Noah's first school was a private Catholic School in Cincinnati. So, he had a Christian background until about the age of thirteen, when he was expelled."

"For what?

"Seems a friend of his wanted to ride around in a car that didn't belong to him and Noah went along. He spent time in Juvie for 'receiving stolen property,' then was transferred to the Ohio School for the Deaf in Columbus."

"How did he end up back in Juvie?"

"He ran away, stole a car, himself, then went to the owner's house to rob it. She was there and he shot her. If that wasn't enough, then he supposedly kidnapped her four-year-old son, even though he released the boy a few miles away at a rest area on the interstate."

"What will he get for that?"

"Well, he's charged with murder, burglary, and kidnapping, although the murder charge may be reduced to manslaughter. Considering the seriousness of his charges, he will probably get life without parole. He hasn't been sentenced yet. But when he turns twenty-one, he'll be transferred here to this facility from Indian River. Of course, if he's tried as an adult, he's more likely to come here sooner. . . at age eighteen."

"I was tried as an adult and came directly to this place, the 'big house.' But I expect he'll have some scary times being here that young."

"You're one of the few 'lifers' who was eager to meet with me," the chaplain said. "I remember it well; you attended bible study and my services."

"Well, I knew I screwed up; I hurt so many people for what I did. My family in Zambia suffered great shame and sorrow in their village. My American missionary family, the Bakers, had to return there without me, and face them with the fact that I had run away to avoid leaving this country. I betrayed the Bakers' trust when all they ever did was give me love." James was quiet for a moment. "I've prayed hard for God to forgive me and vowed to lead others to Him by being an example of His love."

James turned and noticed other men beginning to file into the room and quietly take seats in the first three rows.

"By the time Noah gets to this facility," the chaplain said. "I'm hoping all six rows on both sides of this aisle will be filled with your fellow inmates."

"Keep dreaming, Chaplain. It's hard in here. Some guys are still angry and full of vengeful feelings. But maybe, one day, our message of hope and forgiveness will get through to them," James said in a strong voice. "When you teach, your words are hopeful to those who will listen."

"I'm taking a copy of a study bible written especially for men to give Noah. You can sign it as a gift from you, if you want. If we leave at 10:30 a.m. tomorrow morning, we can be there in time to have lunch with him. The food in Juvie is catered by a local restaurant, actually pretty good."

"Thank you, Sir. I'll be ready. Do I have to wear this uniform?" James laughed, looking at his orange jumpsuit. On the back were large black letters "DOC" for Department of Corrections.

"I'm afraid so, son. But once we're in the juvenile facility, your wrist restraints will be removed. They know I wouldn't bring anyone who is a threat to others or who would attempt to bolt."

"Thank you for your trust, Chaplain," James said with a slight waver in his voice.

The following morning, they made good time and arrived at the facility before noon. Chaplain Beck had his name tag attached to his sports jacket lapel. James was wearing his orange jumpsuit. The men, and the accompanying corrections officer, Sergeant Jeremiah Hawkins, approached the sergeant staffing the visitation counter. The sergeant looked up and smiled when he recognized Chaplain Beck.

Beck smiled back. "Good morning, Sgt. Monahan," he said. "We're here to see Noah Campbell. This is James Abraham, an inmate at Allen-Oakwood. He'll be with me. Sgt Hawkins, here, will release Noah's wrist restraints and remain in this area while we visit Noah."

"Okay, Chap. Just sign both names on the log and give me your photo ID. You know the gig. Place your personal items in the basket on the conveyer belt. I assume your inmate has nothing on him."

"I brought a bible for Noah. Feel free to leaf through it if you're concerned about contraband," Chap responded.

"I trust you, Chap. Just lay it flat next to your wallet and watch. Campbell and an interpreter are waiting in the large visitation room. No reason for you to be couped up in a professional visitor's cubicle." He place two visitors' name tags on the counter between them. "Here are your tags for the front of your shirts."

Beck and James attached them as they walked single file through the metal detector and headed toward the secure visitation area.

"Make yourself comfortable Hawkins, "Monahan said. "Behind you is a vending machine with coffee. The restroom is over there." He motioned to the left.

"Thanks," Hawkins said. He had removed the handcuffs from James and now stuffed them into his back pants pocket.

In the visitation area, Noah was sitting at a rectangular, metal table wondering who had asked to see him. His wrist restraints had been removed so he could sign with the ASL interpreter now seated across from him. He recognized her from a recent interview with his new attorney, Dan Singer.

I think her name is Martha something. She kind of looks like my grandmother, he thought. *Kind of chunky with short, gray hair, bangs, sparkling blue eyes. She wore* small pearl earrings and a navy turtleneck sweater with her name tag attached to the collar. Noah assumed she had chosen that sweater because the temperature in the jail was cool. Around her neck was a silver cross on a long, silver chain. She wore two rings on her left hand signifying she was married. *Or maybe widowed,* Noah thought. He felt a connection to her and some sadness.

The door opened and two men approached his table. Noah stood. The older man dressed in a navy-blue blazer, white shirt with a red tie, tan corduroy pants, and sturdy brown shoes, introduced himself to the interpreter as Chaplain Tom Beck. Noah read his lips. Then he introduced the younger dark-skinned man in prison garb as "James Abraham." Martha introduced herself verbally, then signed for Noah's benefit.

"Noah, this is Chaplain Tom Beck, and James Abraham."

Chaplain Tom greeted him slowly knowing Noah would read his lips. He reached forward and shook Noah's hand. Then Noah turned to James and extended his hand. Martha Dumphy and the three men sat down in the cold, steel chairs. After a few pleasantries, Chap began the conversation.

"I don't believe you've been to a chapel service yet, Noah. We would welcome you there. James attends services and our 'Celebrate Recovery' meetings. You know, James stayed here briefly a while back, but he's now at Allen-Oakwood State Penitentiary, not far from here. He attends my bible study group there. You might be interested in his story. He can share it with you, if you're interested."

"I haven't been to chapel or done anything but eat and sleep, basically," Noah signed. Martha translated Noah's response to both gentlemen.

"Thank you for coming to see me," Noah continued. "The days are long here. My dad visited not long ago. He fired my public defender and got me a really good lawyer. I met with him for the first time yesterday." Noah stopped signing and looked up toward the corner of the room. He sighed and shook his head. Then he looked over at his interpreter and continued, "Then there's my mom. She and my dad divorced when I was little. She visited because she says she wants to be supportive. But that's hard to do when you keep moving around . . . between husbands, I mean." He crossed his arms in front of his chest and shook his head.

James waited a second, then slid the book he had over to Noah. "I brought you a men's devotional Bible, Noah. I received a similar one like this when I was in this facility," he said while Martha signed. "I took it with me to the big house, you know, the men's penitentiary, and it gave me some hope and comfort."

James began to tell his story. "When I was young, I was tried as an adult and found guilty of six counts of murder even though I didn't commit them all. I was sentenced to life without parole and transported to Indian River for two years and then at eighteen, to Allen-Oakwood. That was the worst day of my life," James paused.

"You killed *six* people?" Noah signed. "How did *that* happen?" Martha asked James the question.

"Well, I'm not proud of it, but I got in with the wrong crowd. I came from Zambia in Africa, to stay with a missionary family for a year and attend high school. I loved being in this country so much, in fact, that I ran away to avoid returning home to my village in Africa. That's when my nightmare began. I found the wrong people to hang with, who I thought were friends. I soon learned they weren't my friends." Noah was watching James' lips closely and had understood some of what he had said without Martha's signing.

"When I ran off, I had nowhere to go," James continued. "The Bakers had given me money, an allowance, they called it, for doing chores. I mowed grass, weeded lawns, raked leaves, and shoveled snow. Their daughters and son had chores, too. I kept all of my money under my mattress. The night before they left to return to Zambia, I took a duffle bag filled it with all my stuff, a second pair of shoes and all the money I had saved. I took my high school I.D. and slipped out my bedroom window. But not before I left them a 'thank you' note because I really appreciated what they had done for me."

"You were in this strange country, and you just ran away not knowing where you'd go?" Noah signed with an incredulous look on his face.

"Yes, I took a bus into the city of Toledo and slept on a bench beneath a church overhang. The next day I went into a shopping arcade with a food court. Three guys who looked dark like me started talking to me. They could tell from my accent that I was not like them. You know, American."

Noah smiled. "If they were deaf, they would not have heard your accent." Martha smiled too.

"Yeah, good point. They invited me to their house close to the Greyhound bus station. I had no place to go and I wanted to fit in, so I went with them and took the 'happy pills,' they gave me. Yeah, and they passed me a pipe to smoke. I didn't know anything about drugs or tobacco then, so I just went along. I was scared to be alone and thought all this would make me feel better. I didn't really think about the pain I was causing anyone else. The Baker family had watched me and their children closely and their community of Moss Creek was pretty harmless, so I was new to all this 'other world' and got hooked pretty quickly.

Noah remained motionless. Chaplain Tom spoke up and Martha signed his response. "It sounds like you both feel remorse. Do you know what that means, Noah?"

"Yes, I know what it means, that I'm sorry, and I can tell you truthfully, that I'm very sorry for causing that woman to die and that little boy to lose his mother. I know exactly what it feels like not to have a mother." Everyone remained quiet for a moment. Then the chaplain spoke again.

"I'll be talking to Dr. Rosie Klein, soon. She's the court appointed psychologist who will come see you. And if you think you might like to get involved in our Christian programs when you get Allen-Oakwood, we call it A-O for short, you can be sure I will tell her that. She's going to determine whether you can gain anything from going to rehabilitation. Rehab is not just a word associated with overcoming addictions. It means learning from your past and developing life skills for the future. The Judge will take Dr. Klein's opinions into consideration when sentencing you. Not all facilities have faith-based programs, educational programs, and social skill programs. But A-O does."

"When I was waiting for trial, the wait was so long," James said. "Can we come back to visit Noah again? No one came to see me which would have helped with the long nights."

"Yes, James, I'll bring you back," Chap said. "Over at Indian River, their chaplain retired and I'll be spending one day a week there."

"That would be great," Noah answered quickly.

"Start reading the Book of John, Noah. We can discuss the life and miracles of Jesus when we come again. You will find it comforting."

"What about a journal, Chap?" James asked. "Noah, I can show you why that helps a lot."

"Absolutely," Chap said. "And Noah, call me Chap, too, if you want."

There was a noise at the door and everyone looked as lunch was brought in.

"Well, our food has arrived," Chap announced. "I told James the food in Juvie is better than in the big house. Let's see if I'm right." Martha laughed and signed to Noah.

Noah was surprised that Chap had ordered them food. He didn't usually have much of an appetite, but with company, he felt hungry for the first time in a while. The trays held hot meat lasagna, fresh salad, green beans, a chocolate frosted brownie, and Italian bread with butter on the side. Chap said a short grace without their heads bowed. Noah watched Martha sign what the message of the grace said. His eyes felt moist. It was nice to have good company, really nice.

Back at Allen-Oakwood State Penitentiary, James lay on his bunk processing the meeting he had earlier with Noah. Again, he was grateful that Chap trusted him enough to take him along on a visit to the young man at the Juvenile Detention Center.

I gotta remember to tell Chap about my friend, George Emmanuel's forgiveness, James thought. *I know he'll appreciate it, if anybody would. I forgot to tell him before because I hate rehashing everything that got me jailed.*

Thinking back to his own sentencing hearing, James remembered how Mr. Emmanuel had tracked him down and come to see him. It had surprised James about as much as when Mr. Emmanuel had spoken to Judge Tucker on behalf of two of the victims who had died while James stood by watching his co-conspirator, Marcus Solomon, shoot them. Emmanuel had also asked the judge to forgive James even though it wouldn't change his sentencing. But, perhaps, it would bring him some peace.

Although James had not pulled the trigger, he had assisted in two murders by arranging the setting where two people were executed. He never forgot the terrified looks on the faces of the two people they had befriended, Sam and April, who they turned against on that terrible night.

"I can't forget when Marcus ordered them to turn their backs and get down on their knees. They held hands as Marcus shot them in the back of their heads. I still remember screams from the back seat of the car where the other two girls were watching. I knew I broke poor, Song's heart. She trusted me and I had just helped ruin her and Angel's lives by making them party to murder. It didn't surprise me none that I never heard from Song again after I was sentenced to life without parole. Marcus was sentenced to death by injection."

Yet, when George Emmanuel, the friend and mentor of Sam and April, had come to tell James that he had forgiven him, James could hardly believe it. So many times, James had prayed for forgiveness from God. But he never expected the families of all six victims to forgive him. How could they? But George Emmanuel had.

Then George explained what he had gone through after Sam and April were murdered. He had turned to alcohol which he abused following their deaths to numb his feelings of loss, helplessness, and anger. He had harbored strong feelings of being responsible for their turning to gang life after leaving his protection and before their deaths. But since then, he had completed a Christian twelve-step program and had learned to forgive.

George told James that he wanted James to forgive himself, move forward, and trust his future to God.

George told me that for the past ten years, he had fostered orphans, two at a time, until they would graduate from high school.

Now, he was helping two young men who only had two more years before they would enter the United States Marines. Then, George planned to retire and move to Florida after they did, James thought. *I hope he will.*

"James," George had told him. "I have had you on my mind for thirteen years. The first five, I wanted to strangle you. I got into fights with patrons in my own bar. Then the last five years, I used to fill the dark liquor bottles with water so that when my regulars bought me a shot, I wouldn't get drunk like I had after Sam and April died. Back then, drinking got me into financial and physical problems, not to mention my emotional one's, too."

James simply did not know how to respond. Finally, George had stood up and James watched him walk slowly out the door. He never saw George Emmanuel again, but never forgot his advice: "Time to forgive yourself, James. It's the only thing that helps."

CHAPTER SEVEN

ROSIE PICKED up the phone on her desk in her LaSalle office to call her friend, Linda Willis, and yell: Help! It was a good sign when Linda picked up on the first ring.

"It's me, Linda," Rosie said, knowing her friend would know her voice. "I need help, big time. I have a new case with too many collateral interviews for me to handle. Can you give me a hand, with a few?"

"Most likely. What's in it for me?" Linda laughed. "I work for food, you know."

"Seriously, I have a case where a teenage deaf kid stole a car and went to burglarize the owner's home. She was there and confronted him. He killed her and abducted her four-year-old son."

"Wow, Rosie. How terrible! So sad for the kid. Who do you want me to interview and how?"

"Thanks! For starters, I need you to talk to the directors of his two boarding schools for the deaf. Just call them. They're not located in the Toledo area but Ruth can shoot over their names, numbers, and the brief roles they played in his life. His name is Noah Campbell, age sixteen."

"Okay. Is there a particular subject I should address with them?"

"Well, any brief disciplinary action taken in-house would be a good start. Noah lived at St. Rita's School for the Deaf from the age of five. He got in trouble once at the age of ten. Then at thirteen he was involved in a car theft and spent a year in juvie in Cinci. After that, he was expelled and went on to the Ohio School for the Deaf in Columbus. Long story short, he got in a fight, ran away, and shortly after that is when he committed the murder."

"What a horrible story, Rosie. Want me to look over his medical records for diagnoses or treatments he received as a young child or adolescent?"

"Great idea, Linda. Being a nurse, you'll definitely pick up on his early medical and emotional needs, whether they were recognized or how were they addressed. I'll be interviewing his father. Let me get a release on those records for you and their location."

"Okay, that'll help. So, now I have other news for you," Linda responded in a jovial tone of voice.

"Tell me."

"I'm engaged to a teacher you might know. His name is Frank Flaum and he teaches German in my building. He's divorced about three years now and shares parenting of his son, Klaus, who's twelve."

"Congratulations! How wonderful! When did this happen?"

"Just a few days ago. I was thinking of you when you called. You'll be my matron of honor, won't you?"

"Of course! I'll be honored. Have you set a date?"

"Not actually. We're taking it slowly so Klaus will get used to sharing his dad with me. They are great buddies and usually spend all their allotted time together doing things. They cook. They fish. They go hiking and biking. Stuff like that. Klaus is working on his black belt. Frankie is very proud of him."

"Is that what you call him . . . Frankie? What does he call you . . .sweet cheeks?"

"Very funny. Why don't the four of us meet for dinner this Saturday? He and his ex-wife alternate having Klaus every-other week beginning after school on Fridays. This weekend starts his week off of parenting. You and Bucky will enjoy meeting him. Frankie is into sports so I think the guys will have lots to talk about. And he loves music, especially jazz, so you two will have that in common."

"Sounds like a plan. Maybe we can listen to music after dinner. I'll check our schedule and get back to you. By then, I'll have the contact information for you on the witnesses. Right now, Dr. Luke Campbell is waiting for an interview with me."

"Thanks, Rosie. Give Ruth my best. She's the finest office manager I have ever known. When I arrive early for group, her laugh makes me smile, and I can shake off my negative thoughts."

"You're right, Linda. I'm blessed to have her and I know it. She's been devoted to me through thick and thin. Her own husband isn't in the best of health either, but, she rarely misses work and now comes to the downtown office, too. Once she unlocks an office door, it's as if she has entered her mission field. She leaves all personal matters behind. It's really quite amazing."

"Never thought of that. You hit the nail on the head. Hope

you have a productive interview. Bye. I'll wait to hear from you about dinner tomorrow night with our men."

Rosie went out to the small waiting area to greet Noah's father. She anticipated his fear and anxiety in regard to his son's future.

"Hello, Dr. Campbell. Thank you for coming in today. Did you park in the garage? If so, I can give you a parking pass."

"That's okay, Dr. Klein, and please call me 'Kirk.' I parked down the street by the Juvenile facility. I plan to visit Noah there when I leave. I have permission to take him some clothing , underwear, T-shirts, socks, things like that."

"I won't keep you long today, but I *am* interested in his medical records, and I need your authorization to obtain them. I would also like to hear about his early childhood. I understand that he entered a special needs boarding school at age five, St. Rita's. Is that correct?"

"Yes, I regret sending him away, but at that time, I was working fulltime at the University of Cincinnati and my commute one way was often ninety-minutes or more. Then to supplement my income, I taught classes two Saturdays most months. His mother left when he was four. She couldn't adapt to his inability to hear. Mind you, he was smart. I could tell by how he spent his time. He loved picture books. He liked science books about dinosaurs, planets, or stars in the universe. His pre-school teacher told me he could read."

"I haven't met his mother yet. Did he miss her? Did she visit often? How did she explain to him that she was no longer going to live with him?"

"I have no clue what she told him. He acted out at school a little after she left. He peed the bed for about a year. Dr.

Elizabeth Erickson told me that he was very bright, but confused and angry."

"Dr. Erickson?"

"Yes, she was a child psychologist who I took him to see when his mother left. She played games with him and gave him a chance to display emotions through play therapy."

"What reason did his mother give you for leaving?"

"She was in love with a professor, you see, not really a milkman which is what I tell people rather sarcastically. After I had an affair with a younger undergrad, we divorced. Then we reconciled until someone else swept her off her feet. It hurt Noah mush more when she stopped visiting the second time, probably because he was older by then. When we were first married, she felt stifled by not having an advanced degree. Since then, she has gotten her masters and PhD. I've heard recently that she lives in Portugal."

"Well, enough about her," Rosie said, "how would you describe your relationship with him while he was at St. Rita's?"

"I thought it was strong. Two weekends a month I took him home with me. I had moved from our large, two-story home into a small condo with a second bedroom for him. We visited museums to foster his interest in science. He always hugged me and waved good-bye when I returned him to the school."

"Probably because he trusted you to return."

"Well, I was lonely, and I remarried. We built a house with four bedrooms and a tennis court. After that, Noah showed some real natural talent for tennis. But my new wife couldn't accept my commitment to Noah two weekends a month, so the marriage didn't last. Then I moved to a modest three-bedroom ranch closer to St. Rita's. It seemed strange that he never asked what happened to his stepmother."

"You mean about her not being around anymore?"

"Yes," Kirk said. "But then, I suppose they never really bonded."

"What happened next?"

"Well, when he was ten. He stole some money from the staff vending machines at St. Rita's on a dare from an older kid. He was punished by being restricted to his room for a month, other than going to classes and meals. I didn't get to pick him up during that time either so it was a punishment for me, too."

Rosie nodded in sympathy. "Noah told me he was thirteen when he got into serious trouble. Is that fairly accurate?"

"Yes. He liked basketball, and a local church had a weekly, evening program that included supper and playing ball. I thought it would be a great outlet and opportunity to be with kids who could hear. But I never suspected that the preacher's kid, who they called 'PK.', would be the mischievous one. He stole a car for a 'joy ride' or so he said. But when the cops pulled them over for driving without lights on, PK and the other passenger fled. Noah was sitting in the back seat and got busted. Good thing he wasn't sitting in front or they might have thought he was driving without a license. They also charged him with receiving stolen property. Can you imagine that?"

"I can. Sometimes small things lead to bigger one. What happened after that?"

"He spent a year at Indian River Juvenile Detention Center. After that, St. Rita's wouldn't take him back. It was against their bylaws to have a convicted felon in their facility, even though he had been charged as a juvenile. I guess only two strikes and he was out," Kirk paused a moment.

"After that, I gave up my weekend teaching so I could visit him at Indian River. I stayed at a Holiday Inn Express and saw him on Saturday afternoons and Sunday mornings. There was a chapel service on Sunday, and I attended with him and his friend, Randy Evans. After lunch with both, I headed home. Randy's girlfriend, Joanie, came once a month or so. Other than that, he had no visitors. I knew Randy was important in Noah's life, so we three hung out together."

"Did you say, Randy Evans?"

"Yes, he was another inmate who had been there for three years or so, by the time Noah got there. He helped Noah get adjusted and feel safe among some rough guys. I guess Randy shot his own father when he was fourteen in order to protect his mother and little sister. He was a nice young man who will stay there until he ages out at twenty-one. You can ask Noah, but I don't think he ever had contact with Randy after his year at Indian River."

"Okay. I'll follow up on that," Rosie said without acknowledging that she had been involved in Randy's case.

"Did you consider taking him home at that point?"

"That's one of my biggest regrets, Dr. Klein. That is exactly what I *should* have done. I found out only later that he could have been mainstreamed, even with hearing loss. I found out that our local school system did provide interpreters. But I thought he would be ashamed to have an interpreter in the classroom with him so I felt my hands were tied. The Ohio School for the Deaf was recommended, and that's where he ended up."

"It's my understanding that he did fine there until summer camp. Is that true?"

"Exactly. Some local kids who were also attending were bullies. Noah was protecting one of his younger friends and punched one of the bullies. Unfortunately, it drew blood. A supervisor tried to grab Noah, but he dodged and ran away. At that point, he was only fifteen. By the time he turned sixteen, I had no idea where he was living; and now, this tragic turn of events."

"I am so sorry, Kirk. Was Dr. Erickson the only therapist Noah ever saw or was other counseling available at St. Rita's?"

"Yes, there was. I think you can still reach Dr. Adler through the school. I will sign whatever it takes for you to get those records."

"Thank you for coming in on such short notice. If you want to meet with me again, just call Ruth and she will arrange it, Kirk." Rosie slipped him her business card. They both stood and shook hands. She opened the door and walked him down the hall to the waiting area.

A pleasant man, she thought. *Sometimes, things just happen.*

CHAPTER EIGHT

DAN SINGER APPROACHED the visitation window and reached to sign the visitor log. "Good morning, Sergeant Monahan. Attorney Singer to see Noah Campbell," he said.

"Here you go, sir," the sergeant said, sliding the visitor's pass over to Dan. "Just toss your keys and change into the tray and step through, please." He indicated the metal detector.

Dan retrieved his personal items on the other side and walked to the elevator, pressing the button for the fourth floor. Professionals were permitted to go straight up to the pod in Juvenile without passing through a hallway wedged between two secure doors.

Once up on four, the doors opened to another officer seated behind a desk. That officer had already been notified by Monahan and had efficiently sent for Noah and his interpreter, Martha, a grandmotherly type. They were already seated and waiting in a small, private room with a window in the door.

"Good afternoon, Noah, how's it going?" asked Singer as he seated himself across from his client. Noah read his lips but waited for his interpreter to sign what had been said.

"Okay. I guess. Played a little basketball on the roof earlier this morning after breakfast. The other kids are smaller. It's nice not to be the smallest kid on the block." Martha said as she interpreted Noah's sign language.

"I have been talking to the Judge about your case," Singer continued. "I'm trying to get you charged as a juvenile but the prosecutor keeps bringing up your prior skirmishes with the law."

"You mean like when I broke into the candy machines at St. Rita's?"

"Yes. But more so when you were involved with a stolen vehicle and spent a year at Indian River. The common thread is that you stole another car, which means you didn't learn from your mistake of the past." Singer spoke slowly allowing Martha time to accurately sign his message to Noah.

Noah paused and looked downward. "I can't believe how stupid I've been. I didn't connect the two events until you just told me. Now I'm scared. Do you think you can get me charged as a juvenile? I finally see how actions can pile up and cause big trouble."

"She hasn't rendered her opinion yet. That will happen with you in the courtroom on Monday. Back to the facts, Noah. Did the woman come at you with a knife *before* you shot her? That's very important."

"Yes, she did. I swear!" Noah said excitedly. "It happened so fast. She said something but I don't remember. I just saw her lips move but didn't get it. She probably thought I could hear."

"Noah. They never found the knife. What did you do with it? You didn't take it, did you?"

"It's got to be in that hallway. Please send somebody to search for it. I ducked into a room where her son was watching cartoons. I never thought about the knife. Just wanted to get out of there as fast as I could. My car was parked down the street. I grabbed the kid under his arm and ran out of the house. I don't even know why I took him! I think I wanted to protect him from seeing his mother's body.

Singer paused and looked directly into his young client's eyes. Noah was weeping silently. Martha handed him a tissue from her purse and glanced at Singer waiting for him to say something. He wrote on his legal pad.

"Self-defense will be nearly impossible to prove, Noah. She was five feet two inches tall. You're six feet. I think we need to focus on getting the charge reduced from murder one to manslaughter and being tried as a juvenile. Manslaughter means you didn't intentionally plan to kill her beforehand. You also face the auto theft, burglary, and kidnapping charges."

Martha looked at Noah and Singer saw her hesitate. "Go on, Martha, tell him," he said. "Tell him what an uphill battle he's facing. I feel sorry for the situation, too, but it's our job and we shouldn't get emotionally involved."

Then he stood and said, "I'll see you both in court on Monday. We'll know more about how to proceed after the Judge's decision is made. Noah, If anything comes to mind that you think will help me represent you, jot it down and we will talk again after the hearing, okay?"

Martha expressed the lawyer's instructions to Noah as Attorney Singer knocked on the glass window in the door to be let out. The corrections officer unlocked the door.

Martha stood and faced Singer. "Mr. Singer, Noah just signed: Thank you, Mr. Singer. I appreciate you helping me."

Then out loud, she added, "He is being sincere. I can tell you that. I've translated for many youthful defendants and Noah is the most authentic one by far."

The officer approached Noah and placed handcuffs back on his wrists. Then he took Noah by the arm above his elbow and nodded at Martha and Dan as they all left the room.

"Good morning, Dr. Klein," Sergeant Monahan said. "I heard from Dan Singer that you would be coming to see Noah Campbell. I've already arranged for two interpreters to facilitate your interview."

"Thank you, Sergeant Monahan," she said. As she signed the visitors' log, she noticed Singer's signature. Handing Monahan her photo ID, she hooked the visitor's pass onto her tweed jacket lapel. Then placing her keys, purse, and briefcase on the conveyer belt, she stepped through the metal detector. The buzzer startled her. She stepped back and removed her watch.

"I can't believe I didn't think of taking off my watch. I guess my ring didn't cause the buzzer."

"Happens all the time. Professional visitors are frequently preoccupied with what they're about to do," Monahan laughed. "At least I didn't ask you to take off your shoes."

This time she walked through successfully and retrieved her personal items. Knowing the office of the certified American Sign Language (ASL) interpreters was across the street, she expected one would be with her during all her interviews with Noah. Interpreters quickly walked over whenever notified they would be needed.

"Hello, Dr. Klein," Officer Wise said. "We had to keep the irons on Noah's ankles, but his hands are free to sign. If you have any problems with him, there's a button beneath the table for you to press. Martha Dumphy should be here any minute. Her partner, Thadd Crawford, won't be with her though; he's having a family emergency. Namely, Thadd's wife is having their first baby."

Rosie laughed and nodded. Then she noticed a sturdy, middle-aged woman, professionally well-dressed walking down the hallway toward her. Rosie extended her hand and said, "Good morning. I'm Rosie Klein."

Martha smiled, firmly shook Rosie's hand, and introduced herself. They stepped into the professional visitors interview room and seated themselves side by side across from Noah. He nodded at Martha and glanced at Rosie.

Martha quickly signed an introduction and explanation of who Rosie was and why she was visiting, even though he had been told by the officer who had accompanied him to the room.

"Good morning, Noah," Rosie began. "I've been appointed at the request of Attorney Dan Singer to evaluate you. I've also spoken with your father. Are you willing to consent to this evaluation and my providing a report to the Court?"

"Yes. My lawyer and my dad told me I could trust you." Noah signed, then began reading along as Martha interpreted the consent form Dr. Rosie had placed on the table. Rosie noted that Noah was right-handed and signed the consent and permission to release information form in neat, small, cursive. She noticed his shoulders begin to relax as he placed his hands palm down on the table. Then Noah looked directly into Rosie's eyes.

Most defendants avoided eye contact, Rosie thought and smiled while taking out her legal pad and pen. *This boy has got a lot of good in him. Too bad he's in such trouble.*

CHAPTER NINE

WHEN ROSIE ASKED Noah to describe his childhood, his parents, and his time at St. Rita's, he needed no prompts to tell his story. As he signed, Martha interpreted:

"My mom left us when I was four, but my dad was always there to tuck me in at night. He was smart and caring. To tell you the truth, I didn't miss her after that and thought 'good riddance.' If she didn't want me, then I didn't need her. After that, St. Rita's was mostly okay.

"At ten, I got busted for entering St. Rita's employee lounge after hours and stealing money from the vending machines. Then some big, older kids wanted candy from the machines in the cafeteria. First, they dared me, but then I began thinking about it. When one kid handed me a hammer that he stole from the maintenance closet, I wanted to seem like a macho man even though, I admit, the hammer scared me. But I did it anyway. Then an alarm went off and I was busted. I got grounded to my room for a whole month. No visits with Dad were allowed which was the worst, most embarrassing part."

"What happened next, Noah?" Rosie asked.

"The older boys who basically bullied me into stealing for them were expelled. The other students stayed clear of me. I could attend class but ate in the cafeteria alone. They stared at me. It was horrible. Stealing landed me in Juvie three years ago. Even though St. Rita's was a Catholic place, we all went to a youth group at a nearby Methodist church. They had a basketball team. That's where I met Tommy. I wanted a friend so I started hanging around with him. He was older and the pastor's kid. We called him 'P.K.' He was big and smart. Besides, he could hear. He told me I had a talent for basketball, but now I think he probably thought I had talent for stealing.

"One night, we slipped out of the gym while everyone was playing basketball. Tommy spotted this car with the engine running and thought it would be fun to go for a 'joy ride.' So, we jumped in and took off. But when Tommy heard the police sirens, he jumped out at an intersection before we even pulled the car over. It was crazy! I was trying to get out of the back seat, but got nailed. At least I wasn't in the driver's seat. The car door behind the driver was unlocked and the closest. If those cops had gotten me for driving without a license, I'd still be staring at those ugly green walls at Indian River. The cops just charged me with 'receiving stolen property' or something like that. Honest, it was a 'joy ride from hell.'

"About a month later at the Juvenile Detention Center in Cincinnati," Noah continued, "I was sent to Indian River Detention Center. I will never forget that year." Noah looked up at the ceiling with a smile, then continued signing.

"I made a friend there, Randy Evans. He was at Indian River for shooting his father when he was fourteen. Now, being seventeen, he'd been there awhile, so he protected me. I never really understood why he liked me. And I never told anyone except Randy that I could read lips. We were great at understanding each other. We used some finger signing with private signals. Randy told me he had an older brother who had protected him when he was young, and he just wanted to give back. His brother went into the Marines to escape their father, the family monster. One night, he shot his father as he was coming upstairs in a rage. He said he did it to protect his mother and little sister. Because of that, he was going to be locked up until he turned twenty-one. Randy taught me a lot. He helped me understand why I feel angry so much."

At this point, Noah became emotional and clenched his fists as he began discussing the next two topics which were obviously painful to him. One was his mother's abandonment. The other was when he found out he couldn't return to St. Rita's after a year at Indian River. "It felt like another thing was being taken away from me," he said, his eyes welling with tears. He wiped them with the back of his hands.

Martha and Rosie glanced at each other to give Noah a brief private moment. Then Rosie sat quietly while Noah composed himself again before asking him about other friends.

"My only true friend was Randy. Other kids would use me to get what *they* wanted, like when I broke into the faculty vending machines because they wanted me to, or when P.K. stole the car then abandoned me when the cops pulled us over. But Randy helped me more than any counselor. He taught me how to control my impulses better and how to start avoiding trouble. He told me to just turn my back in uncomfortable situations and walk away. And he said if I couldn't do that, then count to ten and say nothing. After that, I tried hard being respectful to the officers and staff and tried hard not to cause any more trouble.

"Another thing about Randy that I really liked, he was working hard to get his high school diploma and planned to have an associate degree by the time he got out. I was taking Algebra One and he helped me a lot. Don't get me wrong, the algebra teacher was good. He even made sure to face the class even when he wrote on the blackboard, so I could read his lips. That really helped."

Rosie could tell that Noah was smart. He wrote in complete sentences and basically used good grammar. The fact that he took Algebra at Indian River was impressive. She made a note for Linda to check on the validity of his claims of taking Algebra, not causing trouble, and being Randy Evan's friend.

"And there's another thing about Randy that was good. He had a girlfriend who visited him. I liked her. Her name was Joanie. She sent him food packages that he always shared with me. He never told her that he didn't like beef jerky because he knew that I would take it in a heartbeat. He told me to ask my dad for a journal. So, I did and started writing things down. Randy said it was important for me to write about thoughts and feelings every day.

"At the end of my sentence, when I was transferred to The Ohio School for the Deaf (OSFD) in Columbus, Randy promised to stay in touch," Noah paused briefly and looked sad. "But I never heard from him again. Maybe he thought I went back to St. Rita's. But I wasn't. They told my dad there was no way they would accept me back. They said it would set a bad example for the other kids. Maybe they were right."

At this point, Rosie decided to halt further discussion of Noah's crimes until a later interview. She could see that Martha was becoming tired. Because her partner wasn't able to be here today, Martha was doing all the signing for Noah, making sure he understood exactly what was being asked as required by law for all verbal interviews used for legal purposes.

"Martha, let's take a break. I could use something to drink. How about you?"

Martha looked relieved. "Thank you, Dr. Klein." She tapped on the glass window and quietly left the room.

Intending to continue, Rosie wrote on a sticky note to Noah: *Please draw a picture of six people you love doing what they love to do and label or describe each drawing.* She divided the paper into six equal sections and slid the paper and pencil over to Noah.

Noah wrote back: "Do they have to be people, or can I include animals?"

Rosie printed: "Draw whatever has meaning for you."

The first thing Noah drew was a stick figure of his father and himself fishing. His father was large and Noah appeared to be about seven or eight. They held poles and there was a bucket for fish nearby.

Then Noah reached for Rosie's legal pad and wrote: "On weekends when my dad got me from St. Rita's, we fished at the pond across the street from our house. Dad lived in the house with our dog, Rascal. And boy was he ever! You could not leave a sock on the floor without Rascal grabbing it and hiding it under a chair. He slept in my bed, close to my head. I loved that dog."

He slid the notepad back to Rosie.

The second picture Noah drew was of Rascal, a small dog

with long tail, big eyes, and floppy ears. Noah held a ball, and they were outside with a cloud in the sky. Noah looked larger than he was in the first picture. It appeared that he was about to throw the ball.

The third picture Noah drew was of his grandmother cooking. "My dad took me there for Sunday dinner before going back to St. Rita's. I remember the smell of fresh, chocolate chip cookies, really good!" He wrote "Sunday dinner and cookies" above the drawing.

The fourth he drew was of his grandfather's gravestone. Noah was sitting on the ground beside it, holding a flower. He took back the legal pad and wrote on it: "My grandfather died when I was about six. I missed the funeral because it wasn't on a weekend when I was with my father."

Next, he drew a stick figure of himself as a young teenager with an older boy standing beside him. This time he attempted to speak. The words came out softly and haltingly. "That's Randy, my friend at Indian River. He protected me and liked me. He taught me how to control my temper. I should have listened. If I had, I wouldn't be here today, Dr. Klein."

Before drawing a sixth picture, Noah thought for a long time. Then he drew a small X through the center. He wrote on the picture. "I don't love my mother. She walked out of my life. Now she thinks she can walk back in? No!" He broke the pencil in half and hung his head.

"Thank you, Noah," she said softly. "Thanks for sharing your childhood. The next time I visit, would you mind letting me see your journal?"

Noah looked up and nodded that she could. Rosie tapped on the glass. Within a minute, an officer entered the room and handcuffed Noah. Rosie followed them out of the room.

Later that afternoon, resting on his bunk with his arms folded across his chest, Noah mulled over where he had met Martha before. She looked familiar. *She made me feel like this wasn't just a business meeting,* he thought, *more like she knew me from somewhere before.*

Then he sat up and grabbed the journal Randy had given him at Indian River and which he had hidden beneath his mattress. Luckily, he had slipped it into his backpack and had it in the stolen vehicle with him when he was arrested. The arresting officer had returned it to him instead of keeping it with his other meager belongings which they had locked up.

He started writing a letter to Randy, hoping he was still at Indian River:

Hi Randy,

It's me, Noah. How you doing? I hope you get this letter. I think you might still be at Indian River, so I'm giving it a try. I want to let you know what's going on with me and how much I miss our times together.

I really screwed up. After I left Indian River, I transferred to the Ohio School for the Deaf in Columbus. St. Rita's wouldn't take me back because I had stolen before. I don't know if you remember that I broke into the faculty canteen back when I was ten and it was still in my files. I guess what you do at any time really matters.

But I was only ten! I was scared of the older boys and did what they wanted me to do. After that I was quarantined to my room for a month. That's because St. Rita's was giving me another chance to follow the rules. I thought I learned my lesson back then, but I guess I didn't.

• • •

Having you as my friend at Indian River was the best thing that ever happened to me. You protected me and taught me a lot about controlling my temper. I can't thank you enough. I will never know what you saw in me, a deaf kid, or why you looked out for me that year. But I'm glad you did. I want you to know that you made a big difference to me.

But now, I'm in trouble again. I hope you get this letter. You should be getting out of Indian River about now and I hope you and Joanie have a great future together. Please write back soon while I'm still at the Juvenile Detention Center of Lucas County in Toledo. I will explain it all after I know you got this letter.

One last thing. My dad is really a cool guy and stands by me. I probably made you think he was a jerk for putting me in boarding school. But he only wanted the best for me. I understand that now. I really hope you get this letter.

Your friend, Noah

CHAPTER TEN

As Dr. Rosie Klein was retrieving her photo ID and car keys to leave the juvenile detention center, she saw Martha at the end of the hall.

"Martha! Hi. I'm surprised to see you still in the building. I want to thank you. Your translation was extremely valuable. I also sensed there was a connection between you and Noah. Have you translated for him prior to my session?"

"First, you're welcome, Dr. Klein, and yes, I've translated for him earlier today when his new attorney, Dan Singer, came to see him. Usually I'm in adult courts, like family, probate, or criminal. But today was different. You may have heard that my partner was absent because his wife just gave birth. But both of us will probably be assigned to Noah's case and continue together until sentencing. And if I may say, you're pretty thorough with your interviews of defendants."

"Thank you. I would love to hear more about what you do, and please, call me Rosie. Do you have time for a quick bite to eat? I love the chili at the City Club on cold days, and today certainly qualifies, don't you think?" Rosie laughed.

"I would love that," Martha said. "It's close enough to walk, so let's do it. Good thing I brought gloves and a scarf today."

"I need to make a quick stop at my downtown office which is on the way. Why don't I meet you there?"

"Okay, see you there," Martha said with a quick wave.

Rosie walked quickly to the LaSalle Building, took the elevator to the thirteenth floor and entered the office she leased from Dr. Seifer. Turning on the light, she walked through the small waiting room and as she entered her office, noticed a business card that had been slid under the door. Stooping to pick it up, she stuck it into her coat pocket without looking since she was in a hurry. On her desk was a small pile of mail mostly of advertisements. What she was expecting was a hand-delivered package from Attorney Singer containing the discovery packet with Noah's medical records, but nothing was there. Obviously, it hadn't arrived.

Locking her inner office, she also locked the outer office door to the hallway and returned to the elevator. As she pushed the down button, her eyes saw the business card again on the floor. Apparently, it had slipped out of her pocket. She picked it up and read the back: *Call at your earliest convenience.* No name. Just the number on the front that identified the card's owner as Justin Overly, P.I. Curious, she still decided to wait until after lunch to make the call.

Martha was in the lobby of the City Club when Dr. Klein arrived. "I'm looking forward to our conversation, Rosie. I saw the way you interviewed Noah. Very impressive."

The host seated them by a window where they watched people scurrying back to work after the lunch hour. Theirs could be more leisurely since neither had early afternoon commitments.

"Do you eat here often?" Martha asked.

"About once a month," Rosie said. "I usually ask for that little table over in the corner." Rosie pointed over her shoulder to a small round table at the end of the room. "After I order coffee, I'll go over my notes from interviews with inmates. I'm less distracted sitting back there. I'm only in my downtown office on Fridays where I have no clerical help after twelve noon. The rest of the week, I see private clients in Summerhill. That's where my Summerhill office manager, Ruthie, rules my life."

Martha laughed.

"Seriously, she does," Rosie smiled. "When I check in about this time on Fridays, she'll accuse me of 'walking the streets' again. She says the phone rings off the hook about 1:30 p.m. on Fridays. That's when new clients start calling.

"Really? Why does that happen?"

"Well, on my lunch hour, I often shop at Lamson's or Lasalle's department stores after I've had lunch. Professionals who work downtown see me there or at lunch; we briefly acknowledge one another and return to our respective afternoon responsibilities. I think seeing me reminds them to refer clients to me for their various problems.

"That's interesting, Rosie. You must make a difference in many lives, people from all walks of life, I imagine."

"I do see a lot of people who are depressed or going through hard times. But let's talk about you. Tell me how you decided to become an American Sign Language translator."

"It was personal. When my daughter, Molly, was about

four, she became deaf due to meningitis. There were limited resources for her, and I was frustrated. My husband couldn't handle all the time it took to meet her needs. He left us for his secretary and even now rarely spends time with Molly. Back then, I decided to become a certified ASL interpreter at that point to better understand my daughter and to help other families with hearing impaired children."

"So, do you work privately as well as for the agency?"

"When I first became certified, I needed more money to support Molly on my own. So, yes, I did work privately in the beginning. I no longer do. Once she turned fourteen, Molly wanted to become more integrated into the community. She read lips, so she was mainstreamed into a private Christian school. Between her volunteer work and extra-curricular activities, I was able to spend a lot of time with her after work. Today, she's a healthy teenager and enjoys well-rounded activities. Being deaf has never seemed to hold her back. I'm very grateful."

After a leisurely lunch, Rosie and Martha parted on the sidewalk. "Well, I certainly enjoyed our lunch. Hope you have a nice afternoon, Martha, and I hope to meet Molly one of these days."

"Definitely. Do you by any chance ice skate? We skate indoors at the arena on Sundays after church. Molly's best friend usually joins us after she signs at the church service for the hymns. The girls skate longer and certainly better than I do, but I enjoy the hot chocolate and watching them glide around the ice. What makes me sad, though, is that Molly can't hear the music."

"Sounds like fun," Rosie said. "I'll try to join you some Sunday; sounds like a lovely way to spend a chilly afternoon."

On her way home, Martha picked up pepper steak and sweet and sour chicken from their favorite Chinese restaurant. She drove to their cozy home in Ottawa Hills, eager to spend the evening with Molly who was home from college for the holidays.

After placing her purse and keys on the console in the foyer, she kicked off her shoes and headed toward the kitchen with their food.

Molly was sitting on a stool at the island between the kitchen and dining area engrossed in a book and had not seen her mother approach. Usually, Lily, their calico cat, would hop up in front of wherever Molly sat to signal a visitor approaching. But today, Lily barely noticed Martha's arrival. She was sprawled on the shag carpet in front of the gas fireplace in the family room.

Martha tapped Molly's shoulder and signed, "How was your day?"

"Fine, Mom, how about yours? You look tired." Molly stood and hugged her mother.

"Well, I have a few questions for you," her mother signed. "Do you remember Noah Campbell from when you volunteered at the OSFD camp last summer?"

"Yes, I do."

"He's in serious trouble, and today I interpreted for a psychologist who interviewed him at the Lucas County Juvenile Detention Center. What do you remember about him? What kind of kid was he?"

"Oh, wow. I remember that he would stay at the end of the day and pick up junk left on the playground by the other campers. Then, once, when he hit a bigger, local kid who was bullying a little boy, he ran away and never returned. I could relate to Noah, Mom, the bully swung at him first."

"I see."

"And because I'm deaf, I was made fun of behind my back. The kids at school figured I couldn't hear them. But you know I read lips, and I used a little cosmetic mirror in my pencil bag to watch them. I could see what they were saying. Because our last name is 'Dumphy,' they called me 'deaf and dumb.' Some of the boys just referred to me as 'dummy.' It was hurtful. I don't think the teachers knew, or they wouldn't have tolerated that disrespect. Anyway, that's how I know what Noah experienced with bullying and teasing. I felt sorry for him and understood why he acted out."

Rosie had just reached her LaSalle office door when her phone rang.

"Hi sweetie. How soon will you be coming home?" Bucky asked.

"I'm expecting some hand-delivered mail and want to make one phone call before I leave. Then I'll notify Geoff to get my car from the parking garage." She was quite fond of the valet she had known throughout his undergraduate and now graduate school career. "So, what's up that I deserve a call this early in the afternoon?"

"I want you to take a little ride with me. But I don't want to explain and give away the surprise."

"Now you've piqued my interest. Don't you have any meetings or anything at the university?"

"No. I scooted everything to Monday. It will be the last meeting before the holiday break." Bucky was still enjoying his role as athletic director at the University of Toledo and felt heavily invested in the success of the sports programs which generated substantial revenue.

"Sounds intriguing. I should be home within the hour."

Rosie quickly unlocked her office door and saw a packet with a note on a chair in the waiting area. Dr. Seifer had stopped by and happened to be there when a courier delivered it. . She tucked it into her briefcase. *Maybe I'll wait until Saturday to call the mysterious Justin Overly*, she thought. For now, she could tell from the tone of Bucky's voice that he was excited about something. She didn't want to keep him waiting any longer than necessary. This was unusual for him.

As she pulled into their driveway, Rosie noticed Bucky's Jeep Cherokee with the motor running. She shut down her cars motor and entered their front door. As she removed her gloves, Jocko greeted her with a wagging tail and a lick of her hand. Bucky approached with a large to-go cup of coffee.

"It's dark roasted . . . it's black . . . and it's Starbucks," he said. "Just like you like it. Do you need to use the restroom?" Bucky asked after giving her a welcoming hug.

"Depends. How long we will be out?"

"Then, you better make the trip; it'll be a while," Bucky laughed.

Rosie returned from the bathroom and bent down to scratch between Jocko's ears. His big brown eyes looked sad to see his mistress come home and leave again so quickly.

They drove through familiar city streets which meant they were not getting on the highway. Bucky pulled into a shopping center parking lot and stopped in front of a building with a sign that read "Humane Society." He came around and in a gentlemanly fashion, opened Rosie's car door then escorted her through the door into the agency.

"Can you tell me what this is all about, dear?" she asked.

"I think Jocko needs more than human companionship. I would like you to meet Luke."

"Luke? Have we ever discussed this?" Rosie asked.

"I guess not, but it has been on my mind for a long time. There are days when we both have commitments until dark and Jocko is alone all day. Don't you think his life would be happier if he wasn't alone?"

Rosie could only stare at Bucky with a quizzical look.

The humane society volunteer, Mark Stone, brought a dog out to the waiting area on a leash and introduced him. "This is Luke. He has been here about a month."

It was love at first sight. Luke was about ninety pounds, seemed well-mannered and had black with white markings. A pit bull/lab mix, he was curious. Once he perceived no threat from the two strangers, his tail started wagging vigorously and his eyes sparkled.

Rosie couldn't help but pet him. "So, Mark, how did the agency come to welcome Luke?"

"Well, the man who rescued Luke said he was kept on a chain outside twenty-four hours a day, seven days a week. He only had a cage with a blanket over it to sleep in and was infested with fleas and ear mites. It seems like he had never been to a vet, let alone had rabies shots. The owner said he couldn't afford to give Luke the treatment he needed to overcome his physical deficiencies. When he came to us, he was very skinny, but we've been able to feed him so now he's healthy with solid muscles. Just so you know, he is house broken. He was from the very beginning probably because he had never been inside a house. You'll know when he needs to go out. He signals by raising his right ear straight up."

Luke's history brought tears to Rosie's eyes; Bucky looked as if he'd like to meet the guy who rescued Luke.

"Do you have the name of the man who brought him to the agency? We'd like to personally thank him," Rosie asked. She and Bucky glanced at one another, nodding acceptance of their new family member.

After signing papers and leaving the agency, they were both surprised to see how the dog hopped into the jeep through the back hatch without hesitation. Then he sat upright as if he knew he belonged there all along.

"Maybe he smells the scent of Jocko." Bucky said.

"Do you think Jocko will be jealous?" Rosie asked. "Now we'll have one dog sleeping on the floor on each side of the bed," she smiled.

"I think Jocko will be thrilled," Bucky said. "Oh, by the way, I was told Luke snores."

CHAPTER ELEVEN

It was 9:00 a.m. when Rosie, Martha, and Thadd Crawford, her ASL partner, took their seats across from Noah in the visitors' room at the JDC. Noah handed Rosie his journal and signed as Martha interpreted.

"Here's the journal I promised you, but I would like it back, okay?"

"Of course," Rosie said. "I'll return it next time we're together." Noah smiled in thanks.

"Now, will you explain, in detail, how you ended up here, Noah?" Rosie asked.

"Yeah, I screwed up again during the summer camp program at OSFD," Noah explained. "Some local kids were there and they were bigger and stronger than the rest of us. Two of them threatened one of my younger friends. I punched one in the jaw and drew blood. Then I elbowed the guy behind me in the gut. The supervisor tried to grab me, but I slipped out of his grip. That's when I ran away." His look showed he knew it shouldn't have happened. "I doubt they even looked for me," he said, as if that justified it all.

Crawford, back from family leave, took his turn interpreting Noah's explanation.

"For the last few months, I've been staying in a room in a boarding house. In exchange for room and donuts, I cleaned the bathrooms down the hall; I made a couple friends with some high school druggie drop-outs. They taught me how to steal food from convenience stores that had no cameras in the aisles.

"But I got tired of eating dry sandwiches and it was getting cold out. I definitely needed more money. One day, I snooped around the parking garage of a nearby shopping center until I found an unlocked car. It was a dark blue, late model BMW. I took it for a ride and stopped at a gas station with a convenience store. The gas gauge read a quarter tank. I looked in the glove compartment thinking there could be money. Instead, I found the registration of the car with the owner's address. To have that in the glove compartment was good fortune for me, but kinda stupid of her.

"When I saw the address, I wondered why she was shopping so far from home. But I figured there was enough gas to get me to her house. I knew it was a woman because there was a Walmart ID tag on the car seat. It said: 'Misty Matthews,' the same name as on the registration. With the car in the parking garage, I figured she was in the store shopping and nobody would be home. So, I planned to rob the house and take some food.

"When I got there, I parked down the street from her house. There was a tricycle in the front yard so I figured she had a little kid. The screen door on the front porch was unlocked and so was the front door, which surprised me.

That's how I got into the house. It shocked me to see a woman cooking in the kitchen straight ahead. How could she be home if I had her car? It scared me, but I snuck upstairs and snatched a gold necklace and a pair of diamond stud earrings from the top of a dresser in the big bedroom. There was a man's gold chain bracelet, too.

"Then, I opened the top drawer and found a gun. That really surprised me. It wasn't very big, more like a ladies gun, probably hers for protection, or whatever. My heart was beating fast, but I stuffed the jewelry in my jacket and the gun, too, then started heading downstairs. I guess she must have heard me coming down because all of a sudden she was there in the hallway with a kitchen knife!

"That stupid lady lunged at me! I was scared and pulled the gun out and shot her with it. I hit her in the chest. She dropped, and the knife flew somewhere. I remember seeing a rng on her finger and for a second, I thought about stealing it. But, somehow, I couldn't take it off her. I felt that was crossing a line, stealing from somebody you just shot. It wasn't the same as stealing from the top of a dresser. . . not as personal, I guess. But do you believe me that it was self-defense? I didn't plan to hurt anybody. Why did she have to be home?! It was self-defense. *That's* true."

"But, Noah, why did you take the little boy?" Rosie asked.

"He heard the noise and was coming out of the living room where he was watching cartoons. I don't know. Maybe I didn't want him to see his mom shot and on the floor with her eyes wide open . . . with the blood and everything. I picked him up and ran to the car. At least I knew to strap him into the car seat in back. Funny as it sounds, I wasn't really *kidnapping* the boy, I was trying to *protect* him . . . protect him from something awful I just did to his mom. I am *so* sorry. I can't get her face out of my head."

"Well, the fact that you didn't hurt him will help," Rosie said.

"I figured if I left him at a rest area, the State Highway Patrol would transport him to safety. I could tell he was a smart little guy. He knew the names of both dinosaurs he was holding. I liked that. His name was Scottie."

"How do you know?" Rosie asked.

"His name was taped to the back of his shirt, above some letters: E.C.L.C. I guessed the 'L. C.' was probably 'learning center.' That's all I know."

"What happened while you drove?"

"I read his lips in the rearview mirror. He was calling for his mom, then his dad. Then something called a 'yaya.' I don't know what that is. But after that, I just kept my eyes on the road ahead. Didn't want to watch him crying."

"They're still looking for the knife," Rosie said, "so they can corroborate your story about self-defense."

"They should find it in the hallway," Noah signed. "Maybe it's under the narrow bench I saw there. Her purse was on top of it along with her kid's backpack. Their shoes were beneath it on the floor. It's there, Dr. Klein, It's got to be there. It was self-defense. It *was*!"

CHAPTER TWELVE

"HEY, Evans! You've got snail mail. White envelope with a letter on white copy paper. Somebody knows the rules around here." The courier waved an envelope at Randy Evans that had already been opened, searched, and read.

Randy got up from his bunk and grabbed the letter. On occasion, Joanie wrote to reduce his loneliness, but he did not recognize the handwriting on this envelope or the return address. Carefully, he unfolded the paper.

Who could know I'm at Indian River Detention Center, he wondered. Then, sitting back down, he began reading Noah's letter. Soon, he balled his hands into fists and pounded the pillow. He'd had such hopes for Noah, and now he read that Noah was back in Juvenile Detention.

The return address said Lucas County Juvenile Court. *How in the world did the kid end up there*? Randy wondered. *It's a different city in northern Ohio, but if Noah wasn't tried as an adult, he would still likely end up back at Indian River. What gives?*

What Randy didn't know was that when Noah was

released from Indian River, he had not returned to St. Rita's. Randy had wondered why his letters to Noah had come back marked "undeliverable" and why Noah hadn't written him. Now he knew. It had only been a year since he had left. Noah was only fourteen then, and serving just one year, while Randy was serving seven. *What happened,* he wondered.

Whatever it was sounded like Noah would not escape a lengthy sentence. The question was where? If Noah was going to be tried as an adult, Randy vowed that once he, himself, was released at age twenty-one, he would go see Noah wherever the young teen ended up.

What Randy didn't want to think about was Noah going to the "big house" where he would be abused and discriminated against. Being deaf there would be the kiss of death. The guards wouldn't know if Noah was being abused, and higher-ups wouldn't know if the guards were hurting him. Which they would be doing.

Randy felt guilty. He knew Noah looked up to him and if he had kept in touch, he might have been able to keep him from acting out when he was angry. The only thing that helped was reading in Noah's letter that he was still writing in his journal and being thanked for getting him started. Yet, apparently, it hadn't been enough.

In the past, expressing my angry or hurt feelings by writing in the journal helped a lot, Noah had written. *But not this time. Sorry, Bro.* The letter ended there.

"Here's a glass of red wine for medicinal purposes!" Bucky kissed the top of Rosie's head and placed the stemless wine glass beside her on a coaster. "You look engrossed in something important, business or pleasure?'

"Thanks Bucky." Rosie looked up at her husband. "All business, I'm afraid. Remember that deaf teenage defendant, Noah, who claimed he shot a woman after she lunged at him with a butcher knife? "

"I do. What's happening now?"

"Well, he's claiming self-defense because he shot her while she was coming at him with a butcher knife."

"Where did he get the gun?"

"He signed to the interpreter that he got it from the victim's armoire when he was first upstairs stealing jewelry in her bedroom. I doubt he really used the word "armoire," don't you? But that's the word the interpreter, Martha Dumphy, used."

"Based on her use of the word 'armoire,' do you trust that she's accurately translating all the rest of his answers?"

"I do, although I also wondered if he really signed the words 'lunged," "armoire," or "*butcher* knife," Rosie said. "I mean, it didn't alter the meaning of his responses, but it could matter to the attorneys on the case. I'll ask her, the next time we meet. The prosecutor could use these details to suggest to the jury that Noah contradicted his earlier testimony, which meant he was being untruthful."

"Well, while you ponder on such things, I'm going to take Jocko and Luke for a walk," Bucky said as he snapped the leashes onto both dogs' collars. "When I get back, I'll put steaks on the grill." Jocko and Luke's tails started wagging. Bucky wondered if it was because of the walk or the mention of steaks. He rather believed that both dogs were smart enough to understand some human words.

Rosie took a sip of wine. "Okay. I'll take a break and wrap

the corn and potatoes in cellophane. They'll only take twelve minutes in the microwave. Don't let 'the boys' drag you too hard. You don't want to aggravate your tennis elbow." She waved to her little family as they slipped through the patio door, heading toward the walking path behind their property.

Then, deciding to add another reminder to her sticky note collection, she took one and wrote: "No mention in discovery materials of knife found in hallway."

I don't think the appearance of a knife will justify his fatal response, she thought, but for Rosie, it would speak to the honesty of the defendant; it just wouldn't serve as a self-defense plea.

Then she stood, stretched, and remembered to latch the door behind her, never forgetting the time she returned home to find an intruder had entered through the unlocked door and stolen her laptop sitting on the kitchen counter.

The phone's ring cut through the quiet. It was Ruth calling after hours. "What's up Ruthie?" Rosie asked while standing at the kitchen island wrapping corn in cellophane.

"You won't believe this, boss lady, but I stopped back at the office to get an important fax that Dan Singer was sending you. As I walked down the hall toward the back of the building, I noticed your office door ajar. I know you don't keep it locked since anything important is always securely locked in your filing cabinet. But it seemed peculiar. So, I peeked inside and immediately saw your beautiful Kinkade painting was gone from the wall behind your desk! I couldn't help but notice your fourteen-carat gold fountain pen and holder with your name imprinted were also missing from the desktop."

"Oh, no! I'm glad you're okay, Ruth. What else?" Rosie said, dismayed.

"I ran up front to call 911 and exited the building in case

the thief was still on the premises. Right now, I'm standing outside our office while two Summerhill cops and two Lucas County Sheriff's deputies are checking the building. They're also looking for a point of entrance. What's weird is that it doesn't seem like any forced entry so far."

"Really? Anything else missing?"

"Yes. From my area, the wall clock, and trashcan are missing, and from my desk drawer, the scissors, a sharp-pointed envelope opener, paper clips, postage stamps and sticky notes are all gone."

"Okay. As soon as Bucky returns with the dogs, we will be down there. Do the officers need to speak to me immediately?"

"No. They're busy tracking down security footage from the corner traffic signal and Apollo's meats. Just come as soon as you can."

Rosie was about to hang up when she asked: "Oh, Ruth, who was in the building last?"

"Well, I called Linda and she said between 5:00-6:00 p.m., she interviewed Noah's father in the office behind yours. But she also said she walked him to the front door and locked it. Then stayed about twenty minutes to write notes from what he told her about Noah."

Just then, Bucky tapped on the patio door for Rosie to let him and the dogs in. Not wanting to interrupt her conversation, he detached the dogs' leashes and filled their bowls with water. All along he was hearing bits and pieces of her dialogue with Ruth.

When Rosie hung up, she said, "Sorry, Bucky, dear. No steaks tonight. My office was burglarized and I need to head down there."

"Wait, let me drive you. You can tell me everything on the way."

"Thanks. There are two Summerhill police and two sheriff's deputies there with Ruth now. She sounds shaken," Rosie explained. "Hard to believe this can happen in broad daylight in the suburbs."

CHAPTER THIRTEEN

BUCKY DROPPED Rosie off in front of her building and went to park as she approached her office. There she saw officer Keagan whom she knew from patrolling the neighborhood.

"Good evening, Doctor Klein," he greeted her. "Based on what we know so far, it wasn't a random burglary. According to your nurse practitioner, Linda Willis, she locked the door when she left. It was likely an inside job from someone in the building. That means the perpetrator, probably one or more, were already on the premises when she left. They could have been in the restroom or in your storage area."

Keagan, from the Summerhill Police Department, pointed to a building across the street. "We're reviewing security footage from Apollo's meat market over there. Your office manager, Mrs. Wayne, described her car, Mrs. Willis' car, and Dr. Campbell's car. She told us none of those vehicles were parked in front of your double glass doors at the time of the burglary."

A second officer approached Keagan, Rosie, and Bucky who were all standing in the foyer.

"Evening, folks, I'm officer Shapiro; I've been checking footage of the traffic light at the intersection of Main and Harmony Lane, a block from here. This is a short dead-end street so anyone turning onto Harmony Lane would have to have business here or be up to no-good. Two suspicious vehicles turned onto Harmony Lane at approximately 5:30 p.m. One was a tan, Ford leisure van with tinted windows. The other was a dark blue Volkswagen. The Volkswagen parked beside your office. A middle-aged man, wearing a navy-blue sports jacket and khaki pants, and carrying a briefcase, entered the insurance agency next door.

"According to footage from the meat market, the Volkswagen backed out and headed up toward Main Street about 5:45 p.m.. However, the leisure van turned into the driveway beside your office that leads behind the buildings. There's no security back there and the van didn't return to the front of the buildings. Somebody must have driven it behind the buildings and exited from a driveway closer to Main Street. We need to check that intersection for vehicles turning onto Main from Harmony Lane after 6:20 p.m.. That is when Mrs. Willis said she left the premises and the footage from the meat market confirms that Dr. Campbell left at 6:00 p.m. and Mrs. Willis left at 6:20 p.m.."

"I'm impressed with your report," Rosie said. "That's a lot of information. Can I go inside, now?"

"Yes, it's safe for you to take an inventory, Dr. Klein. That way we'll know exactly what items we're looking for. The Kinkade painting and pen set might even be pawned by now. It's strange about the smaller items that were taken; they'll probably never be found," Keagan said.

"Well, thank you, officers. The three of us will take a look and get back to you with any additional losses." Rosie and the others went inside.

With a glance over at the waiting room, Rosie immediately noticed an important item missing: Her mother's latched rug that had been displayed on the wall behind the brown, leather loveseat was gone. That loss hurt more than the loss of the Kinkade which could be replaced. But the rug had been a work of labor and love from her mother whose arthritic fingers had painstakingly completed one row a night for over a year to produce the beautiful 24 x 48-inch carpet.

Rosie put down her mid-afternoon coffee and picked up her office phone on the second ring. "Good afternoon, Rosie," Attorney Singer said. "I just left a meeting with Judge Warren and Marlene Woodridge, the newly-appointed assistant prosecuting attorney. Ms. Woodridge was strongly urging Judge Warren to try Noah as an adult to which I vehemently objected, but to no avail, I'm afraid. The meeting was cordial in the Judge's chambers, basically informal, without a court reporter. I remained calm but firm in my opinion that Noah's prior juvenile record should not impact this decision. He has served his year at Indian River with exemplary conduct. He's also volunteered to work without pay. Besides that, he worked in the facility's cafeteria and washed breakfast dishes several times a week. His conduct has been exemplary.

"But the County Prosecutor's office seems to want to make an example of him to dissuade younger delinquents from offending again. Just because he's deaf doesn't soften their opinions at all. Not that it should, but I think they're being extremely harsh with this young man.

"I hate to tell him that he'll be tried as an adult in Lucas County Criminal Court which means he likely won't serve any time in a juvenile facility. It's really a shame."

"I am sorry to hear that news," Rosie said. "It is frightening to think of him being with those older, violent inmates." She patted Luke and Jocko on their heads, lost in thought for a moment. "I'll recommend that he serve time in a juvenile facility until the age of twenty-one. Maybe we can get someone to listen."

Later that afternoon, talking with Dan Singer, Rosie said, "I plan to report that I found him competent to stand trial, Dan. Will you go over the specific charges with him? Martha Dumphy is an excellent interpreter. I assume she can be appointed to represent him at trial."

"Yes, and regarding Noah, I'll definitely do that," Singer said.

"Actually, Dan, Noah writes very well. I've read his journal and all his written responses to my questions. If you just provide him with a legal pad and a couple of sharpened pencils, he'll know how to ask you questions," she said. "I take it you don't want to take a plea deal, nor are you filing 'Not Guilty' due to self-defense. What are you planning to plead?" Rosie asked.

"I'm not sure yet, nor whether I'll have him testify in his own defense. I'll consult with my partner, Bob Sawyer. Have you met him?"

"I don't believe so, but I seem to recall the name. Perhaps he took a family mediation course from the Toledo Bar Association that I taught. If he was becoming a certified mediator, they're required to take the course."

"You're probably correct," Singer said. "He primarily practices in family court. At times he has cases in juvenile when the parents or family members are fighting, or if the parents are not legally married. As far as I'm concerned, divorce cases involving custody of minor children must be heart-wrenching at times. He'll be able to advise us as to whether it's in Noah's best interest to testify, himself." Singer took a second to think.

"Back to Noah, Rosie. He'll face at least three charges in Lucas County. Since the vehicle theft was in Franklin County, I believe they may drop the charges, especially if he's tried for burglary as well as murder, and kidnapping here in Lucas County."

"Any chance for 'manslaughter?'" Rosie asked. "Have you inquired about the knife she allegedly attacked him with?"

"I'm waiting for a call back from Doug Ford or Rachel Adams, the detectives who were first on the scene. I don't believe they looked beyond her body, but I could be wrong. The house is still a crime scene, so no one from the family has been on the premises. The husband and boy have been staying in Columbus at the home of Misty Matthews' sister.

"I'm going to go with them when the detectives go back to the house and search." Singer said. "I want to see the bedroom where the theft occurred, myself. There could even be a clue left in the kitchen, maybe a holder with a knife missing. If a knife is discovered, it still won't excuse the murder. But you're right that it could reduce the charge from murder to manslaughter since that would make it obvious he didn't plan to take her life."

"Do you know which Judge will be assigned to his case when it's transferred to the adult criminal court, Dan? I assume my report will be provided to that judge rather than to Judge Warner. Or, since I was assigned by Judge Warner, will she pass it on to adult court.?"

"That's a good question, actually, Rosie. Hopefully, a compassionate Judge like Kate Brown will preside. Remember her from the Angel Morgan case?"

"I do. It would be good if she caught this case," Rosie nodded.

"By the way, I've contacted Noah's father and he'll come up from Cincinnati tomorrow for a joint meeting with me and Noah. I'll tell him about the plan to request the charge of murder be reduced, and the charges of burglary and kidnapping also be dropped. But since Noah was found with all the stolen jewelry, and her gun, it's unlikely they'll drop the burglary charges. Tough about the kidnapping, though. I believe that Noah meant no harm to the little boy since he did drop him off at a safe place, not just by the side of the road. That should count for something."

Singer looked at his watch, realizing he had to be elsewhere, and decided to wrap up their conversation. "In his written confession, Noah stated that he took the boy to avoid him seeing his mother's body in a pool of blood in the hallway," Dan said. "That shows compassion. If we plead this out, maybe there won't be a trial. Then the case would go immediately to the sentencing phase."

"What will the victim's family's attitude be regarding punishment?" Rosie asked. "I assume her husband, Ken Matthews and possibly her sister, Nora Douglas, will speak at the sentencing hearing."

"At this point, I'm not sure," Dan said. "Other than Noah, who do *you* need to see yet, Rosie?"

"I plan to contact the principal at the Ohio School for the Deaf, and the camp director. It should shed some light on to why and how he suddenly ran away from camp. Do I need a court order to see Noah at the Lucas County jail? I assume he'll be transferred as soon as they rule that he's to be tried as an adult."

"They know you, Rosie. Just show them the original order that appointed you to evaluate him. That should be enough to get you in to see him."

"Okay. Please let me know when he's booked there, okay? Oh, by the way, will Martha Dumphy be notified, or should I call her? She'll need to know when I plan to see him so she can interpret for us."

"The agency will notify her of the visit, but I can give her a call to meet you there. Her partner is back at work now. It turns out that he and his wife had twins," Singer laughed. "I can't even imagine what his home life will be like now!"

CHAPTER FOURTEEN

Rosie entered their office break room where Ruth was eating lunch. "Hey, Ruth, thank you for picking up our late lunch at Mancy's. Their Greek salads are the best," she said. "Have the police been back in touch with us about our break-in and tracing the leisure van?"

"As a matter of fact, there was a phone message that two detectives will be stopping by with a photo spread for you to look at today," Ruth said. "I told them I was expecting you back for a 4:30 p.m. appointment." She looked at her watch then looked up just as an unmarked police car pulled up to the curb. Rosie turned and recognized Detective Tice of the Lucas County Sheriff's Department as he exited the car and entered their office. She went out to greet him.

"Good afternoon, Dr. Klein," Tice said. "This is my partner, Detective Gorman. If you don't mind looking at some pictures, we have six possible persons of interest to show you."

Rosie invited them to sit in the waiting area and placed

the photos on her lap. Slowly, she paged through each one before looking up. "I'm sorry, I don't recognize any of these people. I see one is a woman. Is she known as an accomplice in thefts around here? That would certainly surprise me since I assumed all the suspects were men." She shrugged her shoulders, and smiled.

"Well, we want to be politically correct these days, so we've included a few women," Tice smiled.

Rosie laughed at his wry humor. "By the way, I've been receiving hang-up calls every evening almost as soon as I get home. It's like the caller knows I've just walked in the door. Who could be watching me?"

"What did his voice sound like?" Gorman asked.

"Nothing out-of-the-ordinary; he speaks kind of quietly," Rosie said. "Once, he actually said he was glad I got home safely." Just then, Ruth slipped Rosie a note stating that her 4:30 p.m. appointment had just called, and cancelled for today.

"Is there a pattern, Dr. Klein?" Tice asked. "Do you stop for errands, or go immediately home after work? Or does it only happen when you've been working in your Summerhill office?"

"Now that you mention it, it does *not* seem to happen on Friday evenings when I've been downtown at my LaSalle office. It's really happens mostly on Saturdays after I've had a support group at Summerhill. I usually do a few errands prior to driving home. This past weekend, I walked across the street to Apollo's and got a roast for this Sunday. Then stopped at Churchill Market for fish to grill." She was quiet for a moment. "I did get a call as soon as I returned home from *there*. So, does that mean I'm being followed?"

"Still hard to tell. They could just be watching the house,

not following you. We'll tap your home phone. The problem is that if the caller simply hangs up, we can't trace it. You need to keep the line open by engaging in a conversation at least for a few minutes. If he calls again, and says he's glad you got home safely, try saying 'Thank you' and continuing the conversation. We'll be aware of the call and will try tracing it if you can keep him talking."

"On the other hand," Gorman said, "if you give us your schedule, we'll have an officer at the corner when you leave here this week. Then we'll see if someone is following you."

Without consulting her calendar, Rosie answered. "I can tell you right now. On Monday through Thursday, I leave the office at 6:00 p.m. Even if I've been elsewhere earlier in the day, I'm in this office for group or individual appointments every afternoon except Friday. As I've said before, calls don't tend to occur on Fridays."

Tice looked at his watch. "We'll have an unmarked vehicle in front of McGarrity's Pub at the corner of Main. It won't be noticeable during happy hour." They could hear Ruth's robust laugh come from the break room as they stood to leave.

"Detective Gorman, are you related to *Bill* Gorman the court bailiff?" Rosie asked. "He's a friend of mine."

"Well, sort of," Gorman said. "We're first cousins, but neither of us claims kinship with the other." He laughed. "We're both competitive, see, and we bet on the golf course every Saturday. Loser takes the winning cousin to the nineteenth hole for a beer. We don't advertise the fact we're related. Don't know why, we just never did, I guess."

Rosie had to laugh. "I've played in charity outings with Bill, usually as the token woman in a group so they can use my drive when it's a scramble contest. At times the women's tee is up about sixty yards closer to the hole. So, it's to their advantage to have me along."

"That's a good one," Gorman laughed. "Well, good evening, Dr. Klein. We'll see you soon. Although, you may not see us. We won't be using a regular patrol car in case you're being watched. To avoid suspicion, it'll be dark green."

"Good night, then," Rosie said as she showed the men out. Then, she called out to Ruth: "If you're ready to go Ruth, I think we should walk out together."

"Sure am," Ruth called back. "Be there in a sec."

As Rosie stood, holding the door partially open, keys in hand, she called out: "This is such a mystery. Why would anyone want my stuff? I wonder if it's someone we know."

Ruth picked up the backpack she used to carry her lunch, and the office outgoing mail. Once thing she had never forgotten their accountant telling her: If she dropped the mail off before and after work, she could deduct the mileage on her tax return. "But you cannot deduct mileage to and from *work*, itself, only *after* your first stop of the day until your last stop." Since then, she always made sure to make the mail drop off her last stop. *I'm a clever girl,* she thought.

A day later, Rosie had just gotten to the office when Ruth said Dan Singer was on line one.

"Good morning, Rosie," Singer said. "You can guess why I am calling; it's about Noah. If you want to see him while he's still in juvenile detention, you need to go this morning. Unless we can convince the Judge to leave him at Juvie, he's likely to be transferred to the County Jail by midafternoon."

"What a shame, but I'm glad you called, Dan; it sounds like a good idea to go see him. I read through his journal after I saw him recently. There's nothing in his writing to suggest he thinks about acting violently or even irresponsibly. So, why would he steal a car? Linda is talking to the director and landlady today. My guess is that even though he's smart, Noah has not developed problem-solving skills that provide him with coping strategies. I think he took the car because he was on the run, had little money, and didn't see a way out."

"But you would think he would have learned from experience," Dan said. "The previous consequence of being locked up for a year should have acted as a deterrent to breaking the law again."

"A lapse of judgment for sure," Rosie said. "But his more serious lapse of judgment was when he resorted to tracking the owner down. By the way, he told me that he left the gun behind at the victim's house because he never intended to use it again. Tell that to the Judge. It might count for his intentions not being malicious toward the little boy he took with him."

"It might," Singer said.

"Well, I'll drive down there this morning, Dan. Is your hearing at one o'clock?"

"Yes. Right now, I'm expecting Dr. Campbell any minute. He's being permitted into the hearing because Noah is a minor. I expect we'll talk here before walking over there together."

"That's not a conversation I envy you having. Dr. Campbell will always have the option of spending Christmas Eve with family. But Noah won't be allowed visits on any federal holidays from now on. So, Christmas Day with family is out for him in the foreseeable future, one that looks bleak for such a young person."

"I heard that Tom Beck, the chaplain from Allen-Oakwood Penitentiary in Lima, visited Noah. He brought James Abraham with him. Since James knows sign language he signed for the chaplain and Noah, allowing them to have a conversation."

"Really. I didn't know that about James. When I was involved with him during the Angel Morgan case, I didn't know anything more than what was brought up at trial. I know that Dr. Susan Dearson evaluated him for competency, but I wasn't privy to her report. James is a bright guy, but also serving life without parole just like Angel. I think it's been about thirteen years since the two of them have been incarcerated. The chaplain must think highly of James to have taken him for a visit with Noah," Rosie said.

"I do remember that James lived with a missionary family before he ran away from his host family. It's likely that his religious beliefs and participation in programs, classes, and services led the Chaplain to see a new maturity in him. I'll ask Chaplain Beck next time I see him about his impression of Noah. I'll also be interested in knowing if the chaplain serves at Indian River."

"Okay, Rosie. I'll get back to you after my hearing this afternoon."

"Sounds like a plan, Dan. Bye for now."

Rosie noticed her other line blinking with a call waiting and picked it up. "Dr. Klein here. Who's calling, please?"

"Hello, Dr. Klein, this is Officer Keagan. I have an update for you. The employees in the offices adjacent to you were all interviewed. One young woman in the music store two doors down saw the Ford van when she was taking trash out to the dumpster. She noticed the van because its side door was wide open, but the van was empty, and she thought that was peculiar. So, returning to her own office, she carefully locked the door behind her."

"That's good news. You probably spoke to Jane Woods. I've met her at socials we sometimes hold for business owners in our block. Did she get a license plate number?"

"She did, and yes, it was Jane. We've already gotten the license number from the traffic light camera at the corner. Only problem is that the van was reported stolen from one of the student parking lots at Bowling Green University and only reported missing last evening. The student who owns it, uses it a couple evenings a week when he drives to work at the Circle K convenience store, so he didn't notice it was missing until yesterday. He checks out and we're fairly certain he had nothing to do with the break-in."

"So, where does that leave us?"

"Perplexed, for sure. We do have one other witness I plan to interview a second time once we hang up. His name is Parker Prescott. He saw two white men in a van turning into the driveway between your building and his. He saw two men through the side window of his office who appeared very young by the apparel they were wearing: Baseball hats, sweatpants, and blue and gold sports jerseys. He figured they were Toledo University students and were moving things for you. But he never noticed the van leaving even though he stayed in his office until eight o'clock that night. Do you know him? He runs the little golf shop on the other side of the driveway. "

"I've met Parker and buy golf equipment from him. Interesting that the van was stolen from a university parking lot. The guys might be students at a rival university trying to cover up their association with their real school. The question remains as to how the van managed to leave our street without being seen?"

"We'll get to the bottom of this, Dr. Klein. I'm sorry to say it doesn't mean your belongings will be returned to you. They could be anywhere by now including any flea market in Ohio, Michigan, or Indiana. Have you turned in a claim to your insurance company yet?"

"No, I haven't. I can put a monetary value on the painting, but not on my mother's handmade rug. Thanks for the update. Let me know if I can help in any way." Rosie's voice wavered and tears welled up in her eyes..

Rosie took her coffee mug and walked down the hall to Ruth's reception area and shared what Officer Keagan had told her.

"Well, Rosie, I've been racking my brain about how that van left the street without a camera catching it. Do you think it's still behind us, hidden somewhere?" Ruth inquired.

"Good point. The Allstate Auction company at the far end of the street has a huge overhead door in back. They store things there until they have enough stuff for an auction. Wouldn't that be clever if the van would still be in there? But would those young guys know the way an estate auction works with multiple clients' items being pulled together? Maybe all of our things aren't gone after all. They could have ditched the stuff that Allstate didn't want as they walked through the field at the end of the cul de sac to a car waiting on the other side Do you think it is worth walking through the field, Ruth?" Ruth laughed and shrugged her shoulders.

"I'll call officer Keagan back and suggest they interview the auctioneers," Ruth said.

"Would you? Thanks, I need to hustle down to the Juvie

center to see Noah in case he's transferred across the street to the County jail. Dan Singer doesn't think he'll be tried as a juvenile but, hopefully, he'll be left at the juvie facility for now until the judge decides."

Rosie returned to her desk and stepped into her black leather pumps. Her closed toe shoes lent a professional appearance along with the skirt she wore that reached just below her knees. A silk shirt under her jacket had a collar and was buttoned to her throat which made the gold cross and chain stand out that she was wearing. On her way out the door, she waved good-bye to Ruth now on the phone, most likely with Officer Keagan.

In the car, she fastened her seatbelt and started the ignition, thinking about the call she had not returned. Hmm? Justin Overly, PI. *How does he know me,* she wondered, *and what was his visit to her downtown office in reference to?* She dialed his number expecting to get a message machine, or a receptionist, which would indicate a well-established business. But, surprisingly, he picked up the phone.

"Hello? Justin Overly here. How can I help you?" His tone was friendly.

"Hi. This is Rosie Klein. You left your card under my office door in the LaSalle Building. How can I help *you*?" she laughed. *That's odd, his voice sounds familiar like I've heard it before.*

"Ah, Dr. Klein. I would rather discuss the matter in person. Would you meet me somewhere for coffee? At your convenience, of course."

"I'm available after twelve noon today. If you're downtown, we could meet at the City Club, or at Denny's on Bancroft near the university, if you're west of town." *I have heard his voice before, I'm sure of it.*

"The City Club works for me, say twelve-thirty?"

"Alright. How shall I recognize you?"

"I'm of medium height with sandy brown hair, horn-rimmed glasses, and am wearing a white shirt and black leather jacket."

"Well, Justin Overly, PI, I have a hunch you already know what *I* look like. Would that be correct?"

"Yes, Dr. Klein. That would be *exactly* correct."

CHAPTER FIFTEEN

At the juvenile facility, Rosie placed her briefcase, purse, scarf, and gloves on the conveyer. She signed the guest register and exchanged her photo ID for a visitor's badge. "Have a nice day, Monaghan," she said to the attendant after retrieving her personal items.

"Thank you, Dr. Klein. You, too. Oh, by the way, Campbell is being brought down to the first floor and Martha Dumphy is already in the room waiting for you."

"Yes, I noticed she and Thadd Crawford, her partner, were already signed in. Thanks." A metal clicking sound let Rosie know the first door was now unlocked. She stepped in and waited for the second door to be unlocked. Then, she entered the area and turned to face Sergeant Hawkins who stood by the visitation room for professionals. He nodded and opened the door, then locked it again behind her.

This interview is not one I'm going to enjoy, she thought.

It was intended to prepare Noah for his hearing and probable outcome, the one they hoped would not occur. Being tried as an adult meant he would most likely stay behind bars for the rest of his life. A parole hearing might occur in the future but only after he would serve fifteen years. He might get that future parole hearing since he was being tried for murder *prior* to the age of eighteen. But with multiple charges against him, it was already doubtful any parole would be granted even in that distant future.

This young man's life already looks bleak, she thought. *How can I get him ready for that?*

"Good morning, Noah," Rosie said as Thadd Crawford signed her greeting. Thadd was taking the first twenty minute shift after which Martha would continue for the next twenty. They would continually rotate for the entire time the interview lasted. Rosie sat directly across from Noah and could tell he was reading her lips even before any signing took place.

What a smart kid. If only he had made better choices in his young life. She was glad he couldn't read her thoughts.

"Good morning, Dr. Klein," Noah answered with his fingers. He appeared agitated.

"You have a hearing this afternoon, and I'm here to answer questions and help you prepare for it," Rosie said.

"I know. I appreciate your help," he signed. "But I know there isn't a lot you can do for me at this point. I just have to face the consequences. Is there any possibility I could serve time at Indian River until I age out?" There was a hopeful look on his face.

"I don't know," she answered, watching his expression. "Did you discuss that with your attorney? What did he say?"

"He said he would push for it. I don't want to go to the 'big house.' I'll be dead meat. And I won't see Randy Evans again because he'll still be at Indian River until he's twenty-one. He's probably already nineteen now. I wrote him a letter this week and sent it there." Noah was still uptight.

"Do you want to say anything to the judge today?"

"What do you think, Dr. Klein? Would it help me if I did?"

"I don't see how it could hurt. Speak from your heart. Tell her you're very sorry for your actions and are prepared to face the consequences. But ask for mercy and ask her to allow you to stay at a juvenile facility until you are at least eighteen, if not twenty-one. Tell her you have always been good with younger kids, and think you could be useful at Indian River. Tell her that your story could 'scare them straight,' so to speak, and turn the younger kids around."

"That's a great idea, Dr. Klein. And every bit true. I wonder if Chaplain Beck ever goes to Indian River, or if he just stays at the Allen-Oakwood facility?"

"If he isn't at Indian River, there will likely be someone else there who performs the same duties. I will contact him if that's where you're assigned. But first, I'll talk to Chaplain Beck, myself."

"When I was there for a year, there was a medic named Dr. Platt. She prescribed a medicine for me that helped with my anxiety and kept my thoughts from floating around in my brain. I need it again. My thoughts are pretty black these days. Dr. Platt brought me granola bars and nuts for snacks. She told me she served in the Army Reserves and that is why there were times she would be called away. Anyhow, I really liked her."

"I'll follow-up on that for you, Noah. One way or the other, we'll get you the medication."

Rosie walked swiftly to the City Club, wondering what Justin Overly wanted to discuss. He sounded as if it was urgent. Glancing into the bar area, she unwrapped her scotch plaid scarf from around her throat but kept the matching tam on her head. Then she spotted him seated in a booth facing the door. His self-description was perfect.

Justin stood as she approached and extended his hand. After greeting, they sat down across from one another. The young, handsome server, whom she recognized from previous lunch meetings, quickly approached them for drink orders. Rosie ordered black coffee and Justin ordered a refill of the same.

"Well, Dr. Klein, I know you're wondering what in the world I want to discuss with you."

"You're absolutely correct, and please call me Rosie."

"I have some information, Rosie, that may be vitally important to your safety," he said, then added, "and you can call me Justin. A potential client came to see me and wanted me to follow you for seventy-two hours."

Rosie raised her eyebrows, but quietly listened.

"He offered to pay me a large hourly fee, plus expenses. He was only interested in your daily routines, particularly during the work week, but told me nothing more."

"What did you tell him, Justin?"

"I turned him down flat which is why I'm talking to you. He's *not* a client of mine so there was no confidentiality established. He didn't describe having any relationship with you or what his interest was in wanting this information. So, naturally, I was wary."

"First of all, thank you for turning him down, and secondly for informing me of any potential danger."

The server returned with their coffee and placed a

container of hot breadsticks on the table. Neither had requested a menu, but both asked for a bowl of the City Club's famous chili with shredded cheese on top. ". . . and a Caesar salad on the side," Rosie added.

"I'll have the same," Overly nodded. "Rosie, I would like to offer my services to watch your back when you leave the office for a while and when you enter your home, if your husband isn't there. It appears this man, or someone he might hire, will be looking at you on the days he wanted me to work for him," Overly said.

"So you think this person is dangerous? Should we work with the police?"

"Well, there's no crime committed, so they might not take it seriously at this point. But I don't like the idea of following a professional woman around behind her back. I don't condone someone simply wanting to know another private person's movements and won't support doing it. For some reason, though, I have a feeling there may be an element of revenge he's seeking. It was a tone in his voice, perhaps something connected to the holidays."

"Sounds like a disgruntled ex-husband who won't be seeing his kids and blames me for it. Perhaps his wife is one of my clients, and she might have let him think I said not to let him have the kids, or something like that. It wouldn't be the first time. Sometimes when there's been a divorce, one parent only gets to see the kids every other Christmas. Or maybe the mother has moved far away with the kids. It could even be that there's a protection order preventing him from seeing them."

"I think you may have hit the nail on the head, Rosie. You might want to look at recent custody cases and opinions that would factor into his inability to see the kids this Christmas. I will also run it by my partner who does family law cases. We can go from there. Right now, the police would have nothing to go on since this man has posed no direct threat by phone or in person."

"Let me talk to my husband, tonight, and see what he thinks about you following me for a week or so. If he agrees, how do we proceed? We, obviously, don't want to be seen together."

"I don't think he's having you followed during the day. I think he's just harassing you by phone at night. Maybe he has a day job and can't do anything until after five o'clock."

"Can you describe him? I might recall if I have ever seen him, especially if there is something significant about his appearance."

"He's young, early thirties. So, the child or children, are likely young. Strangely, he wore a cowboy hat and a black turtleneck under a V-neck, dark brown sweater. He wore denim jeans and brown leather boots and has a thin mustache the same color as what I saw of his hair, light brown. He wore a knock-off Rolex and a class ring."

"Wow, that's a lot of detail. Thank you."

"That's what a PI does, pays attention to detail," Justin laughed. "Oh, he also wore brown leather gloves and a long, suede jacket. We met on a cold evening at the Oregon Pub."

After more small talk, they finished lunch and paid their own tabs. Rosie left the premises first, in case anyone was watching her. She also agreed to call Overly once she talked to Bucky.

Back at work, she called from her inner office: "Ruth, I'm heading home to make some phone calls and relax a little. If you want to leave early, feel free to do so. After all it is the holiday season."

"Thanks, boss. I have a rehearsal this evening with my singing group. We have several performances coming up. If I leave soon, I can stop home for a bite to eat first."

"Good. Let me know where and when you're performing. Bucky and I will catch one of your concerts."

"I'll get you front row seats. We can talk about your options tomorrow. Have a relaxing evening with your special guy."

Rosie left the office now painfully aware that someone – anyone – could be watching her at that very moment. A shudder went down her spine as she hurried to her car.

CHAPTER SIXTEEN

REACHING HOME, Rosie was glad to finally kick off her shoes. She stretched out on the leather loveseat and realized it had been a long day. Tuning into Christmas music on her favorite light jazz radio station, she sipped a glass of wine. Bucky wasn't back from the dog park with Luke and Jocko yet, so she called Linda Willis to ask how her consult went with Dr. Jonathan Snyder, principal at the Ohio School for the Deaf.

I'm glad she agreed to call him, Rosie thought while dialing her number.

"He seemed very cordial and concerned about Noah ," Linda reported. "He claimed that he turned in a missing person's report when Noah didn't return to campus by dinnertime. But then he was told by police that Noah wouldn't be deemed missing until he was gone for twenty-four hours, which Dr. Snyder said seemed ridiculous to him."

"I agree. We know how important those first twenty-four-hours are when it comes to a missing person. What else did Dr. Snyder do?"

"When Emily Ferguson, the summer camp director, notified him that Noah hadn't returned, she also told him she had not witnessed Noah bloodying the kid's nose nor knew what had triggered him to do that. She only knew what some younger kids told her happened after they came running in to see her. They said 'the townies were making fun of two of the little deaf kids. One townie grabbed a little guy by his shirt collar and threw him into the grass. Noah was sitting nearby on a park bench, helped him up, and approached the big guy. Then Noah slugged him in the nose, and the big kid fell backwards, hitting his head on the pavement. That's when Noah ran off and didn't return.' That's what Dr. Snyder told me that Emily Ferguson reported to him," Linda said. "Personally, I think he was afraid the kid was seriously injured, and that he'd probably end up back in Juvie."

"Did Dr. Snyder say anything about the kind of resident Noah was?"

"He told me that he used to spend time with Noah. They took walks and ate lunch outside at a table near the cafeteria. He believes Noah was a victim of bullying at St. Rita's and that is why he always favored the underdog; it was also the reason he was respected by his classmates for defending the little guys. Noah was trying to be his best. He took a martial arts class and an art class. He spent time writing in a journal and hours just reading in the library. He even volunteered in the kitchen. It sounds like he was reliable and hardworking, if you ask me."

"Did Dr. Snyder do anything to try and find Noah, himself?" Rosie asked.

"He said the most difficult thing to do after calling the police, was to call Dr. Campbell, Noah's father, and report Noah missing," Linda said. "Dr. Campbell immediately came from Cincinnati and the two of them combed the woods behind the dorm. Then they both drove around the streets of Worthington looking for Noah, but couldn't find him. That's when Dr. Campbell left him off and headed to the police station."

"Thanks, Linda. Tomorrow, I'll call Noah's landlady and get her impression of Noah. He cleaned bathrooms for room and breakfast, I think, and delivered newspapers to make money."

"Okay, Rosie, sounds good. I'll type up my notes for you," Linda said. "You can check back with me, if you have any questions. Oh, and by the way, it sure is a bummer that your office got robbed. I'm sure the door was locked when I left. Any clues yet?"

"Well, Ruth has an idea that she's going to share with Officer Keagan. You know that auction company at the end of the block? She thinks the van could be parked inside their back warehouse. That's why it was never seen leaving the block. Sounds plausible, right?"

"Yeah, sounds possible."

"We haven't heard back from Keagan yet as to whether they've talked to anyone in that company. Ruth and I heard that if items don't sell at an auction, they're taken to flea markets or craft shows later to be sold. My mother's carpet and my Kinkade painting could turn up at either one of those places. But there are zillions of flea markets, and this isn't the season for outdoor craft shows," Rosie said. "Anyway, I look forward to getting your notes, Linda. Just put them on my desk at Summerhill and I'll glance at them tomorrow. By then we'll know where Noah is going to be held until his trial or sentencing in case they take a plea deal."

Rosie heard a buzz on the line. "Linda, I've got another call coming in. Let's talk again soon."

"Hi Rosie. It's Dan Singer. The judge is going to try Noah as an adult, but will allow him to remain in Juvenile, which means Indian River, until he reaches twenty-one years of age. That's much better than eighteen.

"That's *wonderful* news," Rosie said with a sigh of relief.

"Well, the idea that he left the gun behind influenced her, I think, and the fact that he wants to help younger kids in Juvie by telling his story so they don't end up back there or worse. His testimony was very impactful. I believe we have you to thank for prepping him and giving him the confidence to speak.," he said.

"Thanks for the compliment," Rose said, "but Noah came up with the idea himself. I just inquired about the gun. He said he dropped it so Scottie wouldn't see it in his hand and because he had no need to keep a weapon."

"Yeah, well, that's all good." Dan said. "I also found out that his case is assigned to Judge Kate Brown from the Criminal Division. We're very pleased with this entire outcome."

"I'm really glad to hear that."

"Yes, and now that this phase is behind us, your role will change. Competency is no longer an issue," Dan said. "We'll need to get you appointed for the evaluation he's entitled to before his sentencing. Since we won't go to trial, we'll have to reach a plea deal on the charges with Marlene Woodridge, the prosecutor, even though the penalty will be determined by Judge Brown."

"Okay, Dan. Let me know when and where I should see

him again. I'm glad you called but you are probably exhausted."

"That I am, Rosie. I'll be in touch."

"Have a nice evening, Dan. Again, thanks for letting me know right away."

Rosie heard Luke and Jocko coming down the hall. Both large dogs together sounded like galloping ponies. She also heard Bucky's footsteps following behind.

"Hi Hon. How was your interview with Noah? Bet you have lots more to tell me about your day than I have to share about mine." Bucky kissed her on the head and dropped down beside her on the loveseat.

"More than you can imagine, Bucky," she said placing both hands on his knees. "Do you want me to get you a drink with cheese and crackers?"

"You stay where you are, dear. I'll do exactly that for both of us. Need a refill?"

"Not yet. . . but the evening is young."

Within a short time, Bucky returned with a plate of assorted crackers, sliced Colby cheese and large, stuffed green olives on the side, placing them on the coffee table in front of the loveseat.

"Okay, shoot." He leaned forward, filling a small plate with crackers topped with Colby while waiting for Rosie to talk about her day.

"Okay, here goes: I visited Noah prior to his afternoon hearing. He decided he wanted to speak to the judge. We talked about what he would say, particularly about *how* he should say he was sorry for his actions. Then I met Justin

Overly, a private investigator, for lunch at the City Club. He contacted me first by slipping his business card under my door at the LaSalle office. I returned his call and agreed to meet. I still wonder how I might have known Justin in the past.

"A private eye, huh? What did he want?"

"He said a potential client wanted to hire him to spy on me for several days. He declined and therefore was not bound by a confidential agreement. He wanted to warn me that someone is interested in my routine movements. It all makes sense, Bucky, with the hang up calls that have been happening recently just after I arrive home, don't you think?"

"It does, Rosie, it certainly does. Did he recommend you call the police?"

"No, because the guy hasn't done anything illegal. He hasn't threatened me on the phone, in writing, or in person. He said we could hire him to follow me home from the office and watch the house if you aren't here yet. The police are already watching the office when I leave."

"I think that's a great idea. Better safe than sorry."

"I told him I would call him after I ran it by you. After dinner, I'll do that. He said the guy was interested in weekdays which means my coming and going from the Summerhill office."

"Did he think he was linked to your office break-in?"

"No. He thinks it's unrelated. He thinks it's a disgruntled father from some prior custody case who might not be able to see his child or children over Christmas for one reason or another and blames me. That's just a hunch, but it could be anything, really."

"Well, I'm here now, and so are Luke and Jocko, the best

watch dogs you can find. You know you're safe this evening, don't you?"

She nodded.

"So, I'm thinking steak tonight. How about if I grill them since we didn't get to eat the night of the break-in?"

"Sounds great. I'll work on the corn and baked potatoes we didn't get to eat, too. But first, can we rest a few more minutes and enjoy our wine? Why don't you tell me about *your* day, Bucky?"

"Absolutely, precious. I found we're going to do well in the Mid -American Conference basketball season. The team just returned from a tournament out west and got to the finals. They lost, but their performance was very promising. Looks like our season tickets are going to be very enjoyable this winter."

"I always look forward to basketball season. It reminds me of when I was on the university dance team for half-time shows. One of my most exciting memories was the year the team beat New York University in Madison Square Garden. That was the year New York was ranked number one in the nation. What a thrill for our team to beat them. And just being in New York during the holidays! Then watching the Christmas tree lighting at Rockefeller Center made for a great memory!"

"You did have fun as an undergrade co-ed, didn't you Rosie?"

"I really did. But little did I know my career direction would change so dramatically; that I would leave public education for psychology, in the private sector, no less," Rosie smiled at the memories.

"Okay, Bucky. I'm going to make a quick call to Justin Overly and hire him to watch my back for a few days. Hopefully, whoever this guy is will draw attention and he'll be caught in the act of spying on me."

"Do that. I'll get the grill started and season the steaks. Luke and Jocko can hang out on the patio with me."

Rosie dialed Justin's number who answered promptly. "Justin, this is Rosie Klein. Bucky and I would like to hire you. We agree that your plan sounds viable. How do we proceed and how do you get paid?"

"I'll be near your office at five-thirty tomorrow. Let's talk then. As far as payment is concerned, I'll invoice you. Did you get a call this evening when you got home?"

"No, as a matter of fact I didn't. But then, I came straight home from downtown rather than from Summerhill because you and I met for lunch, so my routine was modified today. That seems to make a difference. Or could he have seen us having lunch together and been frightened away? I can't imagine who would want to harass me; I don't have a single idea."

"Not to worry, Rosie. From this point on, I have your back. By the way, do you recognize me from our high school choir? I was a freshman and you were a senior. I figured you hadn't noticed me then, so you wouldn't recognize me now. But I'm pleased to be able to help.

That's where I know his voice! she thought. "Well, it's good to know you now."

CHAPTER SEVENTEEN

Rosie reached for her legal pad and pen as she listened to the phone ringing on the other end of the line. Then she heard a deep, kind voice answer her call.

"Good morning. This is Chaplain Beck."

"Good morning, Chaplain, I'm Dr. Rosie Klein, court-appointed psychologist. Do you have a few minutes to talk about Noah Campbell? I'm evaluating him for sentencing purposes."

"Of course, Dr. Klein, I would like that."

"Great, thank you. I understand you visited him recently along with James Abraham. First, I'm interested in your impression of Noah, and secondly, why did you take James with you?"

"Easy enough to answer. First off, I found Noah to be a very humble young man. He showed genuine remorse for what he'd done and true shame for his actions. He eagerly accepted the men's devotional Bible I had James give to him. Here at Allen-Oakwood, James leads Bible study. He also learned American Sign Language his last year in high school before he ran away from the missionaries' home. Those are two reasons I chose to take James along with me. Another reason is that I thought it might make Noah more comfortable to have a young person there to sign for him.

"I'm assuming you thought he would be serving his time at your facility. Is that so?"

"Not necessarily," Chaplain Beck said. "Beginning in January, I'll be spending one day a week at Indian River. So, no matter where he serves, I will be seeing him."

"That's terrific! I'm truly glad to hear it. What was your take on the hearing and Noah's testimony?"

"Well, Dr. Klein. I discreetly attended the hearing and sat unobserved in the back of the courtroom. If you had anything to do with preparing Noah, you did a super job. His testimony impacted everyone in the room, right down to Sally Jacobs, the court reporter. I noticed she was tearing up a couple of times as she took dictation during the proceedings. Again, his remorse came across as genuine, as did his desire to help other juveniles if he's permitted to remain at Indian River.

"Do you think he'll remain at Indian River until he ages out?" Rosie asked. "He's being tried as an adult, you know, and Dan Singer, his attorney, has asked that he remain there until age twenty-one."

"Well, it hard to say. I do know what he said impressed Judge Warner. She told me off the record that she never had a defendant offer to help rehabilitate other inmates. So that could help him stay at Indian River until he ages out. I certainly hope so. No one that young needs to be in the Big House."

"The final verdict will be up to Judge Kate Brown in adult

criminal court," Rosie said. "That session will be emotional with the victim's loved ones all testifying on his behalf. I think Noah will likely repeat what he said in juvenile court; he'll express his sympathy and apologize sincerely to the family."

"In my experience, he'll be permitted to hug his father and mother if they're present, then he'll be immediately transported to Indian River."

"I understand. I'll see him once more before that hearing and will tell him we've spoken. I'm also going to contact Dr. Katherine Platt to see if she can start him on an anti-depressant that will help reduce his anxiety.. She's at Indian River and already knows him from the time he's already spent there. Hopefully, she'll prescribe something quickly without having to see him, again."

"That sounds good. I look forward to meeting you at the sentencing."

"Maybe we can have a cup of coffee and you can tell me more about your role in both prisons. I'd like to hear what James is doing. His case and the kids he ran with have been on my mind lately, especially Angel Morgan."

"I'll leave a time in my appointment book for coffee; I'd like to learn more about your role as well."

"Good, then I'll look forward to our next conversation. Until then, have a nice day."

Rosie dialed the Indian River intake office and was greeted by a pleasant voice. "Good morning. Dr. Platt's office."

"Good morning. I'm Dr. Rosie Klein, forensic psychologist, and would like to speak with Dr. Katherine Platt at her convenience. Is she in today?.

"She's currently making rounds, Dr. Klein, but should be in the office within the hour."

"Wonderful. Let me give you my private number and I'll wait to hear from her." Rosie gave her number and as the receptionist copied it down she made a comment.

"Are you calling from Florida? My parents retired to Florida. I recognize the area code."

"Well, I did post-grad work in Florida for three years; that's when I got this cell phone number. Right now, my office is just up the road from yours in Toledo," Rosie laughed.

No sooner had they hung up, and Rosie jotted down a few notes from her conversation with Chaplain Beck, when her phone rang.

"Dr. Klein? This is Dr. Platt returning your call."

"Thank you for your quick response, Dr. Platt. I'm the psychologist appointed to evaluate Noah Campbell for sentencing purposes. Do you remember him from Indian River, and are you aware he's currently facing some very serious charges?"

"I do remember Noah. A nice young man, deaf as I recall. We used a very competent ASL interpreter to communicate with one another. I'm sorry to hear he's in trouble again. I thought he had a good future since he was so young and somewhat a victim of circumstance. Had a lot of loyalty to his friends, too. You know he spent an entire year here because he wouldn't disclose who the driver of a stolen car was. He called it a "borrowed" car at the time."

"I had no idea," Rosie said. "Sounds honorable, but that loyalty ended up costing him incarceration instead of probation, didn't it? Due to his current situation, he has asked me to contact you for an antidepressant to reduce his anxiety for the upcoming sentencing hearing," Rosie said. "Whatever you gave him last time helped and he was hoping you would prescribe it again."

"I have no problem doing that," Dr. Platt said. "Once he gets here, I'll re-evaluate him and determine whether he needs long-term drug therapy or not."

"Chaplain Beck will also provide counseling on a weekly basis. Noah won't have to rely totally on drug therapy." Rosie responded.

"He'll serve time at Indian River until he ages out at twenty-one," Rosie said, "then most likely, he'll serve out a very lengthy sentence at Allen-Oakwood."

"Sad for such a young person. Well, thank you for calling, Dr. Klein, I'm glad I can do something to alleviate his anxiety. I'll send the prescription to our pharmacy if you can arrange to have it picked up and delivered to him."

"I'll do that. Perhaps our paths will cross one day soon. I would like to meet you in person."

"I would like that too. Until then, Dr. Klein."

CHAPTER EIGHTEEN

Rosie stretched her arms overhead and stood up from her desk. She approached Ruth who was on the phone and waited until her jolly, robust office manager hung up and scribbled something on her pad.

"Morning, boss. You got in here early," Ruth said. "Not often that I smell the fragrance of freshly brewed coffee when I unlock the door."

"I had phone calls to make and I'm only halfway done as we speak. I'm going to pour a second cup. Want me to top off yours, Ruth?"

"No thanks. I had a cup on the way and I'm sipping my way through the strong brew you just made."

"Okay, then, back to the grind. By the way, who did you just schedule?"

"His name is Shane Hale. He remembers you from a charity golf outing and wants to see you about issues he and his wife are having. Apparently, she's agreed to see you for couples counseling. I didn't see an opening for an initial interview until a week from this coming Saturday. I hope it's okay to schedule them on a Saturday morning. You don't have a group on that day and he seemed anxious to get started."

"That's fine. I'll talk to you after I call Emily Ferguson, the summer camp director at the Ohio School for the Deaf. I want to know her impression of Noah and her take on why he ran away and didn't return. My last call will be to the landlady at the boarding house he stayed at in Columbus. Her name is Ruby West."

"Okay. Let me know if you need anything, Rosie. I'm spending the morning billing insurance for your clients. You'll be glad to know that everyone has paid their co-pays at the time of services."

"That's nice. Sorry you have to deal with insurance companies that seem to leave you on hold forever."

"That's why you pay me the big bucks, boss lady." Ruth laughed and Rosie waved goodbye as she disappeared into her office.

Now sitting in her comfortable wing-backed chair, she stretched her legs out on the ottoman, then dialed the number on the Ohio School for the Deaf (OSFD) camp business card.

"Good morning, Ohio School for the Deaf summer camp. How can I help you?" a young, pleasant voice answered.

"Hello, I'm Dr. Rosie Klein, and would like to speak to Emily Ferguson please."

"I'll be happy to put you through. What is this in reference to, please?"

"It's in reference to a young man who attended the camp last summer."

There was a slight pause before a woman's voice answered. "Good morning, Emily Ferguson speaking."

"Good morning, Ms. Ferguson, I'm Dr. Rosie Klein, a court-appointed psychologist. I was hoping you could provide information regarding Noah Campbell. I've been appointed by the Lucas County Court to evaluate Noah for sentencing purposes."

"Sentencing purposes?"

"Yes, I'm sorry to say he's been charged with burglary, murder, and kidnapping."

"My word, how can that be? He was such a gentle person, always taking up for the underdog. Are you sure you worded that correctly? Wouldn't you mean 'burglary, *kidnapping,* and murder?"

"No, actually, the order I gave is correct." Rosie went on to explain the case in detail.

"I'm so sorry to hear that," Ms. Ferguson said. "While Noah was here, he ran away after defending a younger boy by punching the bully in the nose. But it sounds as if he has gone way beyond a simple punching situation."

"Did you know him, personally?"

"Yes, I did. Noah volunteered at the camp and was willing to take on any task, menial or large. After events, when the town kids left, he would stay and help clean the picnic area and grounds."

"On the day he disappeared, did you notice him missing soon afterward, or discover why he didn't return?"

"At first, I thought he'd just run off for a while and would return to the cafeteria by dinnertime. The camp day ends at 4:00 p.m. When we took attendance, I reported to Dr. Snyder, the principal here, that he was absent. Dr. Snyder felt the same way I did. We figured he would show up by six o'clock for dinner. But, obviously, he didn't."

"What happened after that?"

"I believe Dr. Snyder contacted the police to report Noah missing, then contacted his father. The police wouldn't make a move until he was missing for twenty-four hours. But his father drove up to school from Cincinnati. He and Dr. Snyder cruised around looking for Noah. Being deaf, Noah was more at risk than most runaways. Honestly, Dr. Klein, it worried me to death."

"You described Noah as gentle and helpful. What else comes to mind when you think of him?"

"Very eager to learn, whether in the classroom or at camp. He could read lips, you know, and he was always looking to learn other skills such as how to administer CPR, for example. He led a sheltered life here at OSFD and probably wouldn't know how to cope in the outside world. He only left campus when his father picked him up for weekend visits or during camp field trips in the summer. He probably was never alone without supervision."

"That's interesting," Dr. Klein said. "You've been very helpful, Ms. Ferguson. If you think of anything else to help develop a profile of Noah's personality, please feel free to call me. Any small detail could be important."

"I'll be glad to help in any way I can." Emily Ferguson sounded truly dismayed.

"I'll tell Noah that we've spoken. It will probably comfort him to know you don't think badly of him, despite what he's done."

"Of course. It you tell him to write me, I will answer his letters."

"I will definitely do that."

While she had been on the phone, Rosie saw other lines light up on several occasions. Now, she buzzed Ruth to see if any calls were important.

"Sergeant Keagan called but said he'd call back. He also mentioned something about having 'probable cause' to search the auctioneer's building, whatever that means. Could he have a lead on the break-in?"

"Maybe, Ruth. I'm going to call Noah's landlady now, then I'll be done interviewing character witnesses. If Sgt. Keagan calls again, please interrupt me if I'm on the phone."

"Will do," Ruth said.

Rosie dialed the next number on her list and was surprised to hear a male voice answer the phone. "Hello. This is Dr. Rosie Klein. Is Mrs. West available?"

"Ya mean *Ruby* West or *Rita* West?" the young man asked.

"I'm not certain. Who manages the boarding house? Ruby or Rita?"

"That's Ruby. Her sister, Rita, is a nurse, but they share the apartment. Gimme a minute. Let me see if she's here. What do I tell her it's about?"

"I'm just wondering if there are rooms available, and what they cost by the month."

"Okay, here she comes into the office now." Rosie heard him yell over to Ruby that she had a call. Ruby picked up the receiver.

"Hello? This is Ruby West. How can I help you?"

"Hi. I'm Dr. Rosie Klein and I'm evaluating Noah Campbell for the purpose of court sentencing. I'm putting together a personal profile and, as his landlady, I need to ask what you thought of Noah Campbell for the time he stayed at your place."

"Well, for one thing," Ruby said, "I couldn't believe it when the cops came and took Noah away. He had to leave his belongings behind which was only a small pile of clothes, his books, a Bible, a jacket, and a pair of spare gym shoes. What kind of trouble did he get into?"

"Well, unfortunately, before he came to your boarding house, he ran away from the Ohio School for the Deaf. Then he did get into some legal troubles. However, you have been very helpful. Can you tell me more about how he acted while staying at your place?"

"Well, he cleaned bathrooms, swept halls, and took trash out in exchange for donuts, coffee, and a room. My sister and I had him over for Sunday dinner several times. Nice, gentle fellow. He could read our lips. He loved fried chicken and mashed potatoes."

"So, no money was exchanged for his room and board, I take it. He said he had a morning paper route to earn spending money which I assume he used to pay for his other meals."

"That's right. He had a microwave in his room and used it to heat lasagna and other frozen dinners. I let him use our laundromat without paying. He was a real good worker. Are you saying he's a *minor*? We thought he was at least eighteen and saving money for school."

"Well, no, he was a minor and I really appreciate your input, Ruby. If you have any other thoughts to share, feel free to contact me. Do you have an email address? I can send you my contact information."

"Sure. It's my name at gmail. What should I do with all his stuff?"

"I'll check with his father and see if he wants to pick up Noah's personal items. If so, I'll have him call you. Thanks, again, Ruby. Have a good day."

"Oh, wait! My sister, Rita, wants to speak to you." Rosie heard some scrambling noises before a new voice came on the line.

"Hi. This is Rita. I have to tell you what an honest young man Noah was. Ruby allowed him to have the master key to all seven of our rooms. When somebody moved out, he took the old linens to the laundry room and put fresh sheets and pillowcases on the beds.

"Honestly, he had opportunities to steal, for sure, but we trusted him. Mostly, I was impressed about him knowing CPR. People stereotype deaf kids as stupid, but Noah was bright and wanted to succeed. What on earth coulda *happened*?"

"That's a great question, Rita. Thank you for your input," Rosie said. "As I told Ruby, feel free to contact me if you want to share other thoughts about Noah. Oh, one last thing. How did Noah deliver the papers?"

"He had a bike. He kept it in our storage shed in the backyard. Sometimes it was too cold for him to be on that bike in the early morning, but one way or the other, he had to pick up his papers two miles away. I never saw a young person work so hard. He never complained either. Ruby made sure he had coffee or hot chocolate and donuts when he got back from delivering."

"Did either of you notice if he had a vehicle the last time you saw him?"

No, not as I recall. Maybe it was parked a few houses down, if you say he had one. Lots of college students park on our street and walk the half mile to campus. We just don't know."

"Well, again, thank you and have a good day, Rita. I told Ruby that Dr. Campbell will contact you for his son's belongings."

"Okay, Dr. Klein, bye. Say 'hi' to Noah from us, if you see him."

CHAPTER NINETEEN

THERE WAS a tap on Rosie's office door, then Ruth brought Dan Singer in behind her. "You were on the phone, Boss, so I didn't want to interrupt. Attorney Singer is here to drop something off but he wants to talk with you."

"Good morning, Dan," Rosie said. "To what do I owe this pleasant surprise? Care for some coffee?"

"That would be nice."

"What do you take in your coffee?" Ruth asked, "and Boss, want a refill?" Rosie shook her head no.

"Just black, thank you," Dan said. Ruth left to get the brew, then returned with it moments later.

"Well, Rosie, getting right to the point, Detectives Adams and Ford found the knife under a hallway console," Singer said. "It has the victim's fingerprints on it and no others. Nor was there any blood. So, they assume she was holding it and it fell from her hand when she landed on the floor after he shot her. Which doesn't help our case much, except it validates Noah's statement that it could have been self-defense; only who can say if she lurched at him."

"Do you think she did? Even if she warned him to leave, he wouldn't have heard her," Rosie said. "But he might have read her lips," she said, second-guessing herself.

"I don't think so. Noah might need to believe it was self-defense to live with himself, but most likely, she startled him, and he acted impulsively. If she said something, he wouldn't have heard her. But her suddenly appearing in the hall probably did it. The other thing is that he dropped the gun *before* he grabbed the boy. That could mean one of three things: He didn't want the boy to see his mother lying there, he really didn't plan to use the gun again, or I think he panicked and ran with the boy before he thought about anything at all."

"Well, that's interesting. I'll certainly add the possible panic point to my report."

"On another note, Rosie, I asked my partner, Robert, whether he's heard anything in family court about a distraught, threatening father possibly following you. He told me that most men blow off steam, but never pose a direct threat to anyone. I would look in a different direction, if I were you."

"That's okay, Dan. I have a PI helping me now. . . Justin Overly. Do you know him?"

"Know him. . .I've used his services more than a half-dozen times. How did you happen to connect with the best PI in the local area?"

"He contacted *me* after some guy wanted me followed. Since he didn't like the feel of the case, he called to warn me after he had turned the job down. Bucky and I agreed we should have *him* follow me for our own reasons, namely my safety, so, we hired him."

"You're lucky to get him. He doesn't take every job that comes along because he's not in business for the money. A couple of years ago, his seventeen-year-old son was killed in a drive-by shooting. They never found the shooter. His kid had been scheduled to play football at the University of Dayton that fall."

"What a tragedy! How did it happen?"

"He was leaving the field house at Whitmer High School and walking to his car with three teammates. They were all killed. It devestated the parents, as you can imagine."

"It's hard for any parent to lose a child."

"Back then, Justin was with the Toledo Police Department, Internal Affairs. He wasn't a popular guy because he busted dirty cops. After that, he felt responsible for his son's death and wonders if his son was targeted as a message to *him*, that maybe the other kids were collateral damage. His wife worked in the school library and never set foot in the building again. Justin left the force and went into private PI work trying to find the shooter, himself, but he never did."

"I am so sorry to hear all this," Rosie said.

"One way or another, you'll appreciate his work," Dan said. "Well, I'm due in court in half an hour, so I'll take off now." He put his empty coffee cup on the side table and stood as Rosie opened the door and walked with him to the reception area.

"Bye, Ruth," Dan said. "Thanks for the coffee."

"My pleasure, have a nice day."

"Ruth, please hold my calls, will you?" Rosie said. "I really need to get on this report."

"No problem, Rosie. You may have five sticky notes on your door, but I won't allow any visitors or phone calls to interrupt."

"Thanks. I can always count on you."

Officer Keagan arrived at the office and saw Rosie's car. Although he wanted to bring her up to date on his investigation, Ruth, steadfastly refused to allow him to interrupt her boss. An hour later, when Rosie emerged from her office, that was the first sticky note she decided to address. After getting a coffee refill, she returned to her desk and dialed his number.

"Officer Keagan. It's Rosie Klein. Sorry not to have met with you. Do you have information for me?"

"Yes, I do. We found the van in the auctioneer's warehouse. Your Kinkade painting was gone, but your mother's hooked carpet was still in the back of the van along with some small items from other nearby offices. I think you had a hunch kids were involved, right?"

"Based on the office items they took, it seemed like amateurs, for sure. After you said the van was stolen from a Bowling Green University student lot, it made sense that someone familiar with the driver's schedule could be involved."

"A guy named Harry Logan, an auctioneer, gave up two young guys right away thinking he could make a deal with us. It didn't work. When we picked up the thieves, they turned on him and told us that Logan pays them once a month to grab a vehicle and rob an unlocked office. Since they don't break in or use a weapon, it's not considered 'breaking and entering.'"

"Really? I'm still wondering how my office was

unlocked," Rosie said. "That's not likely. Something else is still off."

"Not really. The one kid confessed to being in your waiting room as if he was there to see Linda Willis. He used the restroom and never came out. No one usually checks bathrooms before locking up, so it was easy to come out after everyone else went home and rob the place."

"Well, that's pretty brazen. Teaches a lesson, doesn't it? But why did they steal the small stuff?"

"Well, the kids said Logan let them keep incidentals as long as anything of value was brought to him. We recovered other valuables reported stolen from small businesses in your area. As for you, it wasn't personal. It had to do with your location, particularly the driveway beside your office that led to the back of their warehouse."

"Well, I find it rather strange that this Logan let the van stay so close to the scene of the crime, meaning near my office, with most of my stolen items still inside. Don't you think that's rather naïve of him?"

"Maybe, or just a slip up on the part of the kids. See, the way Logan worked his system was that by putting on multi-residence auctions, he would receive items from homeowners for his auction, but would also mix in a lot of stolen office things in besides to make having possession of them seem legit. Then, after any auction, he would pay the homeowners what he owed them minus his commission and would pocket what he made off the stolen items when they were purchased. Since nobody knew who owned what, it was the perfect cover for fencing stolen goods.

"Usually, paintings are fenced pretty quickly," Keagan said, "Sorry about your Kinkade, but he probably got rid of that right after your items were stolen. And because of the way his auctions were held, all outside our jurisdiction, the Lucas County Sheriff's Department was also in on the bust. They'll be the ones handling the fine print, meaning the reports."

"Well, that's an incredible twist of fate for me to get my sentimental items back. I would have hated to tell my mother that her hand-hooked carpet was stolen. I can't thank you, and Sergeant Shapiro, enough. I should also thank Detectives Tice and Gorman, too."

"They may be in touch before closing out the case. But for now, just relax and enjoy your evening. Someone will be returning your items soon enough."

"Thank you. I'll let Ruth know, and we'll start checking the bathrooms before leaving at night. She and Linda have been skittish about being in the office alone since the robbery. This will help a lot. 'Night, officer."

CHAPTER TWENTY

As Bucky walked out the front door to pick up dinner for Rosie and himself, Justin Overly's car was parked just down the street from their townhouse facing in the opposite direction. Overly was watching through his rearview mirrors and saw Bucky lock the front door before leaving.

Inside the house, the phone rang. Rosie picked it up and heard a male voice say: "Glad you're home safely."

"Thank you," she said, trying to engage him in conversation as instructed so the call could be traced. "I appreciate that you care." She heard a click. He had ended the call.

How interesting, she thought. *He doesn't want to talk at all, just wants to scare me. . .have control over me. Imagine that. Or maybe he realized I was trying to keep him on the phone so the call could be traced. He's smarter than I thought. Or maybe he spotted Justin Overly watching the house.*

She picked up the extra cell phone Justin had given her – a burner phone – to call him and report the hang-up. "Hello Justin. I just got a call."

"Okay, Rosie. Nobody out here looks suspicious, no vehicles parked, nor pedestrians walking by the area. If this guy knows you're home, he's either in another house watching or could be using some sophisticated long-range equipment. But the fact that he called just *after* Bucky left the house makes me think he's *watching* from somewhere nearby. Has your house been swept for hidden cameras since this started?"

"No, I don't think so," she said.

"We'll have to get that done right away. This guy is ahead of us and we've got to catch up."

The next day, Dan Singer greeted Rosie as she arrived at his office mid-morning. "Thank you for your evaluation report on Noah, Rosie, especially since you've hand-delivered it," he said.

"You're welcome. I'm taking a copy to the prosecutor's office next. I wouldn't want Marlene Woodridge to accuse me of playing favorites."

"If you have another copy for Judge Warner, I'll be seeing her later; be happy to deliver it."

"I'd appreciate that very much, Dan. Here it is, and a copy for Judge Brown, too. I'm in a bit of a hurry so that'll help me a lot. Will you let me know what your thoughts are after you review it?"

"You can bet on that."

Rosie left Dan's office and hurried out into the cold, brisk air. Pulling on her gloves, she wrapped a wool scarf around her neck to cover her mouth against the cold air since it was a two-block walk to the Lucas County Juvenile Court Building. She entered the building, went through security, and took the elevator up to the third floor. When she exited, the reception area was straight ahead.

"Good morning," she said, smiling at a young woman seated behind the counter. "I'm Dr. Klein and I'm delivering a report to Marlene Woodridge."

"I'll be glad to take it, unless you want to speak to her personally."

"Thank you. That won't be necessary, but I appreciate you handing it to her," Rosie said still smiling. As she handed over the manilla envelope and turned to leave, the young woman called after her.

"Dr. Klein? Do you remember me? I'm Jennifer Frost. You interviewed me when I was ten years old to determine which of my parents should have primary custody of me and my little brother."

"Oh, my goodness, Jennifer!" Rosie said with true surprise. "I *thought* you looked familiar, but your name tag says: Jennifer *Sullivan*. How are you? How's your family?"

"Everyone's fine. My mother and father were granted shared parenting, thanks to your recommendation."

"How did that work out?"

"It worked great. We spent Monday and Tuesday nights with my mother and Wednesday and Thursday nights with my dad. Both lived in our school district, so school wasn't an issue since one or the other would pick us up. We spent every other weekend in one household or the other."

"How did you decide which parent had Monday and Tuesday versus Wednesday and Thursday?"

"You won't believe this but since most tests are on Friday, and my dad was better at math, they agreed he would be better at preparing us for tests on Wednesdays and Thursday nights. Since then, they've both remarried other partners whom we really like. My brother, Jon, lives mostly at Dad's since it's closer to the University. He's there studying pre-med."

"That all sounds wonderful, Jennifer, thank you for sharing. How are you, personally?"

"I'm very happy, and married to Patrick Sullivan. We met in law school at the University of Toledo which I'm still attending. We're both in our third year. My husband is interested in family law. I'm going to practice criminal law and start as a public defender. I don't usually sit at this desk but the receptionist is out ill today. How fortunate though since I recognized you right away."

"What do you usually do?"

"I'm a girl Friday, running reports between offices and helping soothe victims of crime."

"So, will you be attending the Noah Campbell sentencing hearing when the victim's family and loved ones speak to the judge?"

"Yes, I'm scheduled to be with Judge Kate Brown for the next month, beginning next Monday. I will be seated with the witnesses, Ken Matthews, and Nora Douglas during that hearing."

"That's perfect. I'll be there as well and look forward to seeing you then, Jennifer. Best wishes in the pursuit of your law career." Rosie leaned forward, extending her hand. Jennifer stood, shook it firmly, and smiled at the woman who had given her a new direction in life.

CHAPTER TWENTY-ONE

ROSIE'S LANDLINE phone was ringing as she entered the house. Hoping it wasn't her phantom caller, she answered to hear Dan Singer's familiar voice.

"Hi Rosie. Your report was more useful than you can imagine," Singer said. "However, Judge Brown won't allow you to testify about anything your character witnesses told you regarding their knowledge and relationships with Noah. She said that's all 'hearsay' and that your testimony will be strictly limited to your *own* direct examination, clinical opinion, and any mitigating factors you may have found.

"Having said that," he continued, "at least Judge Brown read all the statements made by Noah's father, his principals, camp director, medic, boarding house manager, and her sister. I can't believe it won't make some impression on her personally."

"Do you think their opinions will factor into her sentencing recommendation?"

"Their comments are not supposed to matter in court, but

it's similar to when a witness or attorney says something the judge deems inappropriate, and the jury is advised to disregard the statement. You know it's next to impossible for a juror to 'unhear' something. Well, it's extremely difficult for a judge to disregard something he or she has read, as well."

"I understand. You read it, didn't you, Dan? What do *you* think of the witnesses?"

"They make up as complete a character witness profile as I've read in a long time regarding a criminal defendant. And remember, Rosie. I can ask any of them to personally testify, which, by the way, I'm seriously considering doing. I won't bring in a hostile or reluctant witness, only someone who sincerely wants to help Noah. Their testimony will follow yours. I doubt that Ms. Woodridge will cross-examine them.

"As far as prosecution witnesses, you can bet that Ken Matthews will address the court and possibly Nora Douglas. I've heard a rumor that Misty Matthews' own parents are alive and may be attending, too. It's possible one of them may also speak."

"What purpose do you see *my* testimony serving?"

"Unlike a trial phase where experts are called to help determine cause of death, and so forth, your testimony will help confirm that he is not a threat to society, and that it was most likely a random act. Even though he can't get around the fact that he planned to burglarize her house, which was his *intent,* he was not planning on shooting Mrs. Matthews. Your report will show that he reacted on the spur of the moment. It was an emotional impulse most likely based on fear. He saw the knife and perceived a serious threat. He didn't enter the house with a weapon. He didn't leave the house with the weapon.

"The fact that he rashly carried off Scottie Matthews, obviously without the boy's consent, then realized his error in judgment quickly after that, he chose a safe drop-off place in terms of the strong likelihood of the State Highway Patrol would be called and the child rescued without harm. Since that is exactly what occurred, it helps make the case that Noah is remorseful and unlikely to re-offend.

"Despite his deafness, your findings conclude that he is smart, and has great potential for rehabilitation. This means he can re-enter society and do something productive with the rest of his life. That's what your report and testimony can do to help him and it's very good, Rosie.

"You will be the only expert witness and Marlene Woodridge will stipulate to your credentials and your report. She's made the plea deal which is a feather in her cap as far as professional recognition. Burglary, voluntary manslaughter, and abduction of a minor. She knew if she went for murder one, we would battle it out at trial. Hopefully, Noah's terms for these offenses will be served concurrently."

Bucky came through the door as Rosie was hanging up the phone. She noticed he had a big smile on his face. The dogs were brushing against his legs as if to say, "pay attention to us. It's our turn." Rosie approached her little family, greeted her husband with a kiss, and knelt to pat Luke and Jocko.

"Want to walk them with me, Rosie?"

"Yes, I would like to do that. Give me a second to change into something more comfortable. I can't wait to share my recent conversation with Dan Singer. Are you able to be in court to hear my testimony?"

"Of course. Keep your eyes on me and you won't be nervous. Everything is mostly agreed upon, at this point, isn't it?"

"Yes. The hardest part will be listening to the poor family of the victim. I always hate to hear their heartache. No sentence is ever harsh enough when you have needlessly lost a loved one."

They headed out the back way and turned down a side street. In the distance, they saw Justin Overly's car parked in its now familiar spot.

"By the way, speaking about losing a loved one, I was talking to another coach at school who knows Justin. He told me an interesting fact about him. It seems Justin doesn't take every job that comes down the pike and isn't in the business for the money."

"I've already heard the story from Dan Singer," Rosie said. They spent the next few moments talking about Overly's loss.

"Somehow, he thinks it was his fault his son was killed because of his own line of work. He still wonders if his son's murder wasn't a message to *him*. Who can live with that kind of guilt?" she asked.

"Since then, it's destroyed his family life, I heard," Bucky said. "His wife used to work in the school library but hasn't set foot in that building since it happened," Bucky said. "I understand they didn't have any other children and his wife turned to alcohol and prescription drugs to cope."

"Well, this won't go any further and I don't think we should let him know that we're aware of it, do you?" Rosie asked.

"Not unless he brings it up, or wants to talk about it."

"Well, I'm glad we both know about it." she said. "But it

won't go any further from me, either. But it helps me to know the man a little better. He's very serious and seems so dedicated to his work. I guess now we can understand why."

CHAPTER TWENTY-TWO

WATCHING FROM THE SHADOWS, the hidden man saw Rosie clearly through the front windows of her townhouse, just before she closed the blinds. He raised his cell phone to call her when he saw movement on the walkway as Bucky entered the front door.

Home unusually early tonight, aren't you? he thought. The interruption caused him to look down the street. *Hmm, that same car is there.* He had first noticed it two nights ago, but tonight seemed more than just a coincidence. Slipping back into the shadows, he knew he could wait a little longer. His dark clothing blended into the foliage along with the back-pack he had brought along. The one with a long rope hanging from it. Tonight, he had planned more than just a phone call.

Justin Overly had been parked near the Walker's townhouse for more than an hour. He also saw Bucky come home earlier than usual. As part of his surveillance routine, he had parked in a different spot each night to avoid being noticed by anyone watching. But every spot had a clear view of their front door. Tonight didn't seem any different, except that Bucky had come home earlier than expected. Overly was preparing to pull away for the night when he saw the front door open again and Bucky come out with both dogs on leashes. He watched as they walked down the street.

I'd better stay 'til he returns, Overly thought. *No use heading home since she's alone again.*

Not long after that, he felt a sensation he had felt before. His car seemed to slowly resettle into a lower, tilted position on the passenger side of the vehicle. Getting out to check, he walked around the back of his car and noticed the right back tire was flat and bent down to check it. He never heard a sound but felt a presence behind him just before his world went black.

Sitting in the living room, Rosie had just finished reading a report for tomorrow's hearing when she heard a noise in the kitchen.

"Bucky?" she called out. "Are you home already?"

She got up and headed toward the direction of the noise when Bucky walked in the front door, both dogs hustling slightly behind him, tongues panting from their exercise.

"Rosie? Here we are. What's up?"

"I thought I heard you in the kitchen just now. There was a noise."

"No, I'm here, but let's go check."

The dogs bounded ahead in search of their water dishes when Jocko made a slight whimper.

She rounded the corner and saw him holding up his right front paw.

"Jocko, what's the matter, boy? Oh, he's cut himself, Bucky," she said. "Look, there's glass on the floor!"

Bucky came around her and immediately noticed shards of glass scattered on the floor near the dogs' water dishes. One pane in the back door was jagged and broken.

"Someone just tried breaking in. Look at this." He walked over to the water bowls.

"This is getting serious," Rosie said. "There was no phone call tonight, Bucky, but I think we almost had a visitor."

"Let me call Justin," he said just as they heard a knock on the front door and the phone ring at the same time.

"Rosie, Bucky, it's me!" Overly's voice was unmistakable. "I'm at the front door; are you okay?"

Bucky opened it to find Overly looking disheveled and holding the back of his head. "I was knocked out while kneeling by my flat tire."

"We had a break-in," Bucky said, "but whoever it was, fled when the dogs came into the kitchen."

"Looks like our perp is taking things up a notch," Overly said. "I'm going to stay outside tonight so you can both get some sleep. You have a big court date tomorrow."

CHAPTER TWENTY-THREE

THE SENTENCING - PART I

It was just after eight the next morning when Rosie entered the courtroom through the double doors in back and nodded at the officers standing on each side of them. She took a seat in the last row behind the press and noticed her favorite investigative reporter, Wes Hall, to her right in the row in front of her, his notepad open. He glanced over at her and smiled.

I'll ask him later if he knows Justin Overly and if they have ever collaborated on a case, she thought.

Across the aisle to Rosie's left were two middle-aged women who could pass as sisters. Each had shoulder length hair pulled back over their ears and held with dark brown barrettes. They both wore colorful, holiday silk scarves around their necks. Beside them was a gentleman dressed in a navy suit and an attractive, younger woman with long, dark wavy hair and oversized horn-rimmed glasses. They appeared to be together, but Rosie had no idea who these spectators were or what their interest was in Noah's case. It wouldn't be long, however, before she would find out.

Attorney Dan Singer came through the doors with his partner, Robert Sawyer. Rosie recognized Sawyer from her most recent class. She thought highly of Dan Singer for bringing his partner along in the rare event he would not be capable of completing his part of the hearing. *It's good that Dan is cautious,* she thought, remembering a lawyer who once had an acute heart attack in the courtroom. With no back-up present, the case had to be postponed.

The defense attorneys proceeded to the front of the courtroom, took their seats on the right side of the aisle, and placed their heavy materials on the table. The prosecutor, Marlene Woodridge, was already seated at a similar table on the left of the aisle. Her materials were spread out neatly and she looked calm as she waited for the proceedings to begin. A male colleague sat beside her. Positioned in the center aisle was a podium.

Two rows behind Ms. Woodridge was a couple wearing all black who were sitting quietly, their hands folded. The gentleman's dark suit complimented a black dress with a matching jacket that the woman was wearing. Apparently, they were going to speak on behalf of the victim's family.

Stern-looking Bailiff Gorman opened the door on the right and Noah Campbell was escorted into the courtroom by a Sheriff's deputy. He was seated between Attorney Singer and Attorney Sawyer. Noah was wearing an orange, v-neck jail jumpsuit with a white tee shirt beneath it. He wore rubber sandals with socks. His hair was trimmed short and combed neatly. He wore no handcuffs or shackles. He was not considered a flight risk and he needed his hands to sign with the interpreter, who was Martha Dumphy. She stood below the

Judge's elevated bench in front of the defense table, where Noah could see her translations. She would sign everything that was said during the hearing, including Noah's statement to the Judge and the victim's family.

The row behind the defendant was kept clear. In the third row sat Dr. Kirk Campbell, Noah's father. He was wearing a navy blue V-neck sweater, light blue oxford button down collar shirt, and a dark blue bowtie.

The court reporter was to the left of the podium, facing the audience and prepared to record the entire hearing. The deputy returned to the door where he could clearly watch the defendant. Bailiff Gorman called out: "All Rise." Judge Kate Brown, dressed in a black judicial robe, entered the courtroom and took her seat at the bench. The bailiff then instructed everyone to be seated and remained standing to the left near the door to the judge's chamber.

"Court is now in session," Judge Brown said loudly. "No cameras will be allowed to record. Attorney Woodridge, you may proceed with your opening statement."

"May we approach the bench, your honor?" Attorney Woodridge asked.

"Yes, you may," Judge Brown affirmed.

Both Marlene Woodridge and Dan Singer approached the front of the bench since both sides would be privy to anything one or the other would say to the judge. Attorney Woodridge said something quietly to the Judge, inaudible to the audience, and Attorney Singer nodded his head in apparent agreement.

Judge Brown then spoke to the courtroom: "It's the Court's understanding is that the prosecutor's office and the defense team have reached a plea agreement. Is that correct, Attorney Singer?"

"Yes, your Honor."

"Attorney Woodridge, you may proceed with a statement of the agreement, so that it can be recorded for the record. Then we will continue with the statements of the witnesses as called forward by the attorneys. Lastly, it is my understanding that the defendant, Noah Campbell, wishes to make a statement as interpreted by Martha Dumphy. Is that correct, Attorney Singer?"

"Yes, your Honor."

The prosecutor stood and approached the podium. She adjusted the microphone to her petite height and proceeded. "The Lucas County Prosecutor's Office representing the State of Ohio, and the defendant's attorney, Daniel Singer, have agreed to find Noah Campbell guilty of first-degree manslaughter in the death of Misty Matthews. He is also guilty of burglary, commission of a crime with a deadly weapon, and abduction of a minor child." Attorney Woodridge returned to her seat at the table.

"Is that your understanding Attorney Singer? Does your client understand and agree to the stated charges?"

Attorney Singer approached the podium and readjusted the microphone to his height. "Yes, your Honor. We also respectfully defer to the Court as to recommendation of sentencing for the commission of these criminal acts."

"I would like to hear from the defendant," Judge Brown said. "Please have him stand and I ask that his interpreter remove the microphone from the podium to translate his response."

Martha spoke while she signed to Noah: "Please stand, Noah. Judge Brown saw that I signed the agreement to you as it was stated by Attorney Woodridge. Now the Judge would like to know if you understand and agree to the plea arrangement established between Prosecutor Woodridge, representing the State of Ohio, and your defense attorney, Daniel Singer. I will translate your response."

Noah stood and walked to the podium. "I understand the agreement and I accept it," he signed to the judge who looked at Martha who spoke the same words clearly out loud.

"Attorney Woodridge, you may call your first witness," Judge Brown said.

Attorney Woodridge turned and beckoned to Mr. Ken Matthews, husband of the slain woman. Mr. Matthews came forward and faced Judge Brown at the podium. For the first time, Rosie noticed he had a mustache. As he adjusted the microphone with his left hand, she also noticed he wore a large gold watch.

It looks like a Rolex, she thought. *Wonder how many he owns since Noah stole one from his house during the robbery.*

Matthews used his right hand to turn pages as he read from a prepared statement. "I am Ken Matthews, your Honor. My wife, Misty, was needlessly and brutally gunned down in our home by this man, Noah Campbell. Our family will forever suffer from the loss of this vibrant, loving and gentle woman.

"Our son, Scottie, currently grieves the loss of his mother and can't understand why she has not returned from the hospital. Scottie is having traumatic nightmares in which this man is the monster. He dreams of being snatched out of the living room by an evil stranger and dumped at a rest area with no coat to protect him from the cold. He will grow up without his mother and, being such a young age, will have few memories of her.

"I strongly disagree with the plea agreement. This young man should have faced charges of murder and stealing a vehicle in addition to burglary and abduction. Justice has not been served. I strongly urge the Court to sentence him to the *maximum* sentence possible and to serve them *consecutively* in a maximum-security state prison. Thank you, your Honor for hearing the position of our family."

Mr. Matthews replaced the microphone to its holder and returned to his seat with his head lowered. His sister-in-law patted his shoulder as he sat down. Then Attorney Woodridge called another name and the sister-in-law stood up, slung a purse over her shoulder and approached the podium with no notes from which to read.

"Your honor. I am the sister of Misty Matthews. My name is Nora Douglas. My brother-in-law and nephew have suffered a tremendous loss, as have I. It was a shock to find my sister's car missing from the mall parking garage. Yet that never can compare to the feelings we have had to deal with since the thief found Misty's home from the registration in the glove compartment. He drove all that way to rob her house and kill her. For what? A few items of jewelry to pawn for dope money? He should never see the light of day. Let him spend his life not only deaf but restricted to solitary confinement in a dark, damp cell. That is all I have to say."

Nora wiped tears from her cheeks. The sound of the microphone could be heard as she bumped against it on the podium. She turned, glared at Noah, and walked quickly out of the courtroom.

Attorney Woodridge stood and addressed the bench. "We have no other witnesses."

"There will be a thirty-minute recess," Judge Brown announced. "Court will re-convene at ten-thirty." She rose and left the courtroom. Bailiff Gorman called out: "Court dismissed." Everyone filed out except for the defendant, his interpreter, his defense team, and the Sheriff's deputy. Attorney Singer whispered over to Martha Dumphy that he was stepping out to speak with Dr Klein prior to her testimony.

Rosie was standing at the end of the hall, looking out the window. *There's something bothering me about Ken Matthews. . . something peculiar.* Then it came to her. *It's his voice.* She had no previous contact with Mr. Matthews, yet his voice had sounded familiar. Not seeing Singer, she decided to take the elevator down to the lobby and make a quick phone call to Justin Overly.

"Justin, this is Rosie," she said when he picked up her call on the second ring. "Is it possible for you to come over and listen to my testimony? There's someone in the courtroom I'd like you to observe."

"I figured there would be a break prior to you testifying. Am I right?"

"Well, I'm calling you during the break. The father of the deceased is a man named Ken Matthews. I think it's his voice on the threatening calls to me. Plus, he has a mustache and I'd like you to watch him, even tell me, if you can, if he's the man who wanted me followed."

"Actually, I saw him again waiting at the bus stop near the corner of your Summerhill office. He looked like a businessman wearing a topcoat and carrying a briefcase."

"That makes sense; my street is a dead end. He could see me from there when I leave and I wouldn't notice him since he looks like a few other people waiting for the bus."

"Do you think he'll stay for the rest of the hearing following your testimony?"

"With a plea deal, the Judge might do the sentencing before lunch. I think he'll sit through the entire hearing," she said. "If he thinks she won't sentence Noah until later in the day, I think he'll return at that time."

"What's your hunch, Rosie?"

"We have my testimony, a few character witnesses speaking, and Noah. I think we'll finish up later this morning but, Judge Brown won't sentence him until later today."

"Okay, I'll sit in the row with the press and keep my head down so he doesn't"t recognize me. If I'm spotted, he'll think I'm with the press. When you break for lunch, I'll follow him to see if he tails you. Where do you think you'll go for lunch?"

"I plan to meet Bucky at the City Club. Why don't you join us?"

"Only if he's not following you. Remember, he knows me. If I don't show up, you'll know he's somewhere in the vicinity, okay?"

"Yes. I'm really hoping he goes to lunch with his sister-in-law and he has no further interest in me. I'm afraid if he hears my testimony, he'll resent me for appearing sympathetic or something."

"I am on my way."

CHAPTER TWENTY-FOUR

The Sentencing - Part II

Everyone stood as Judge Kate Brown reentered the courtroom from her chambers. Then Bailiff Gorman announced: "Court is in session." Rosie looked around and spotted Justin in the back and Bucky already seated near the middle of the room behind her. She noticed Ken Matthews and his sister-in-law had returned to their seats as did other spectators from earlier.

"You may call your first witness, Attorney Singer," Judge Brown announced.

"Your honor, the defense would like to call Dr. Rosie Klein to the stand." Overly moved to the back wall where he could keep his eyes on Ken Matthews.

Rosie walked forward and stood in the witness box to be sworn in by the bailiff. Placing her left hand on the Bible, she raised her right-hand palm facing forward.

"Do you swear to tell the truth, the whole truth, and nothing but the truth, so help you God?" the bailiff asked.

"I do," Rosie responded, feeling the weight of the moment, she knew the importance of truth. She sat down on the hard wooden chair with her report in front of her.

Attorney Singer approached the bench and asked her to state her name, profession, and what her role had been in this case. Martha Dumphy began signing to Noah.

"Initially, I was appointed by the Court to evaluate Noah Campbell for competency to stand trial. Once it was determined that he would be tried as an adult and an agreement was made between the State of Ohio and the Defense, my role changed," she said. "At that point, I was to provide mitigating factors to the judge for purpose of sentencing."

"Your Honor," Singer began. "We, the Prosecutor and I, have agreed to accept Dr. Klein's credentials as an expert witness and her report as her testimony. However, I have a few questions to ask Dr. Klein to assist the Court in sentencing this defendant."

"You may proceed, Counselor," Judge Brown said.

"Dr. Klein, have you met Martha Dumphy prior to this hearing, and if so, under what circumstances?"

"Yes, I have," Rosie testified. "Martha Dumphy is one of two interpreters assigned to translate conversations held with the defendant or in the presence of the defendant. According to Ohio law, a person diagnosed as deaf by a medical professional is entitled to a certified American Sign Language interpreter at all times. This would be the case in prison or during legal interviews and proceedings."

"In your professional opinion, Dr. Klein, is Noah Campbell completely able to understand the process of this hearing, the consequences, and all the conversations and testimonies? Other than the disability of being deaf, is he of average intelligence? Can he read and write?"

"Noah should have no difficulty understanding the proceedings today, including the testimonies. Despite being deaf, he has above average intelligence. He reads and comprehends at a post- high school level. He writes very well with a good vocabulary and correct grammar. He suffers from no mental illness that would impair his abilities."

"Would his mental health and these academic skills be relevant to rehabilitation in prison?"

"Yes. He is quite capable of completing high school, a post-high school degree, or skilled trade."

"Lastly, in your professional opinion, Dr. Klein, is Noah Campbell a threat to society."

"No. Noah has a personality that tends to want to protect the underdog. He was bullied as a child and typically has gotten in trouble due to standing up for younger children."

"Did he carry a weapon to the home of Misty Matthews with the intent to kill her or anyone in her family?"

"No. He had no weapon and has never owned a weapon. His judgement and reasoning were temporarily impaired, and he reacted impulsively to his unforeseen circumstance. He took the pistol *from* the Matthews bedroom and, after using it, he dropped it on the floor. He abducted the child to prevent the child from viewing his mother's body. He left the child where he believed the State Highway Patrol would take him home safely."

"Thank you, Dr. Klein. No further questions."

At this point, Attorney Woodridge stood at her table and addressed the witness. "I only have a few questions, Dr. Klein, on behalf of the State of Ohio." She walked closer to the witness box.

"We trust your professional opinion. Both the prosecutor's office and defense attorneys frequently request your appointment by the Court on criminal cases. So, let me ask you, what makes you think that *this* young man, who *shot* someone, is not a threat to society?"

Rosie cleared her throat. "I believe that Noah has never learned how to deal with emotions such as fear, anger, or sadness. But he is perfectly capable of developing skills to overcome those feelings and replace them with appropriate responses. I believe that he impulsively acted out of fear, not anger, when he shot Mrs. Matthews. He recognizes it doesn't excuse his actions. If he is permitted to remain in a juvenile facility until he ages out, he will have the opportunity to participate in counseling and take anger management classes to develop better coping skills. He can get his high school diploma, and an associate degree. He has already been visited by a chaplain who will meet with him each week and help guide him toward more appropriate responses to stress. I have been in touch with a medic who will temporarily prescribe antidepressants to enable him to focus and learn. He has shown remorse and expressed a desire for self-improvement. I do not believe he is a threat to society."

"Thank you very much, Dr. Klein. That is all."

"I have a question, Dr. Klein," Judge Brown said. "Do you have a facility in mind for his incarceration and rehabilitation.?"

"Your honor, Indian River is where Chaplain Beck and the medic, Dr. Katherine Platt, provide services. The defendant would also receive the services of Indian River's full-time American Sign Language interpreter who would sit in his classes to assist."

"Thank you, Dr. Klein. You may step down," Judge Brown said, excusing her from the witness box.

"Your honor, the defense would now call Dr. Jonathon Snyder to the podium."

Dr. Snyder quickly walked to the podium and positioned the microphone according to his height. "Your honor, I am the principal at the Ohio School for the Deaf, in Columbus Ohio. I have a brief statement to make on behalf of Noah Campbell."

"You may proceed, Dr. Snyder," Judge Brown answered.

"Noah Campbell became a resident at our school at the age of fourteen. He had previously been a resident at St. Rita's School for the Deaf in Cincinnati. He was shy, lonely, insecure, and needy for a friend. He has a very committed father, but because of Dr. Campbell's work schedule, he was only able to take Noah two weekends a month.

"Noah volunteered to help the staff every chance he had. He worked in the kitchen and on the grounds in good weather. He tended to stay around younger students who appeared to look up to him. They too, were deaf, of course. He did very well in math and science. He was taking Algebra Two and Chemistry. It appeared that he would be a candidate for Gallaudet University in Washington D. C. It is a highly accredited school for the deaf.

"Noah was involved in our summer camp that included kids who lived in town. Nor did we restrict it to deaf kids only. Some were hearing impaired, but not to the extent of our residential students. One day, a small group of town kids were bullying a ten-year-old residential boy. Noah stepped in to intervene and the leader took a swing at him. Noah punched him in the nose. The kid fell backward onto the black top and Noah could see that his nose was bleeding. Noah fled and never returned to the dorm. In my opinion, he was afraid he would get sent back to Juvenile Detention. We called his father who arrived and helped us search for him.

We would not have turned him in to the authorities for the infraction, but he was not found.

"I am here to say that if Noah would have been found at that time, he would have been welcomed back and none of this would have happened. It has been an unfortunate cascade of circumstances. Thank you for listening."

Dr. Snyder returned to his seat as a young woman sitting beside him approached the podium. She introduced herself. "Your honor, my name is Emily Ferguson. I am the Ohio School for the Deaf camp director. I just wanted to support what Dr. Snyder has said in his description of Noah. The boy he hit was not injured. I think Noah assumed the worst and feared he would be expelled.

"He had already served a year at Indian River for being influenced to go on a joy ride by a boy he perceived to be a friend, actually the son of the pastor at a nearby church. As a resident of St. Rita's School for the Deaf, Noah played basketball on Wednesday nights at the pastor's church. When the pastor's son stole a car, Noah sat in the back seat. As police pulled them over, the boys in the front fled leaving Noah alone. For that reason, Noah spent a year at Indian River basically for not telling police who the driver was and who the other passenger was in the car. St. Rita's rules would not allow Noah to return there because of a prior incident of having hit another boy. That is how he came to our facility.

"From the start, Noah was very helpful to me and other camp staff. He showed no aggressive or inappropriate behavior until he was prompted to stand up for that little boy. He has acted impulsively, and we are saddened by this tragic turn of events." Ms. Ferguson left the podium.

Judge Brown announced, "Court will be dismissed until

1:00 pm at which time I will hear the remaining witnesses." She stood and abruptly left the bench.

At precisely 1:00 p.m. Bailiff Gorman entered the Courtroom and announced," Court is now in session." Judge Brown took her seat on the bench. She said to Attorney Singer, "you may proceed with your witnesses."

One of the middle-aged women Rosie had noticed earlier, walked quickly down the aisle, and stood close to the podium. She leaned forward and placed the microphone close to her mouth.

"Good afternoon, your Honor. My name is Ruby West. I own a boarding house in Columbus and Noah Campbell rented a room from me for about two months. He cleaned bathrooms and halls in exchange for a room and breakfast. My sister and I had him for dinner on Sundays because he became so special to us. He could read our lips. He had a paper route and to distribute the papers he rode an old bike someone left here. It became so cold, we worried how he would be able to go two miles to pick up the papers and then deliver them on dark, winter mornings. Never, your honor, would we have expected him to steal a car and go all the way to that lady's house for money. There is nothing he wouldn't have done for us. We felt like he thought of us as his aunts. We were not aware that he was only sixteen. I don't know what we would have done. We don't rent rooms to minors. There are college kids who do rent rooms on our block. We would hate to see him in prison with older men who might take advantage of him both because of his age and his deafness. That is all I have to say on behalf of my sister and me."

Attorney Singer approached the podium. He said, "Your Honor, the defendant would like to address the Courtroom and all who are present here today."

"He may proceed, Attorney Singer," said Judge Brown.

Noah stood in place between his attorneys. His interpreter, Martha Dumphy, removed the microphone from the podium and faced him in order to repeat out loud what he was about to sign.

"Your Honor, I would like to thank you for hearing my testimony. I want to extend my deepest apology to the family of Misty Matthews for causing them such unbearable sadness and pain. I didn't mean to hurt anyone when I entered their home, let alone remove the little boy against his will. I can understand why they want me to pay for what I have done, and I agree that justice should be served. I am prepared to accept whatever the Court finds reasonable.

"I am asking the Court to allow me to stay at Indian River until I age out at twenty-one. I have always been good with younger kids, and believe I could be useful to them at Indian River. My story may serve to 'scare them straight.' When they hear the poor decisions I have made, what I have done, and the resulting consequences I bear, they may think twice before they violate the law themselves. With the education I can obtain there, I will also be able to help other inmates at the State prison, particularly those who are hearing-impaired, to improve their reading and earn a GED. Those with lesser sentences than mine could return to society with skills to lessen the likelihood of them returning to prison. Again, thank you, your Honor for hearing my testimony and thank you to Mrs. Dumphy for translating my words through these hearings."

Noah sat down. He clasped his hands together in front of

him, closed his eyes, and offered a prayer for forgiveness and strength. He turned to look at his father who nodded with a slight smile. *If my father can forgive me,* he thought, *maybe there is hope.*

Surprisingly, Judge Brown spoke in a weary voice. "The day has worn on. Sentencing will be pronounced tomorrow morning at 10:00 a.m. Court is adjourned."

She quickly removed herself from the bench, entered her chambers, and shut the door. Bailiff Gorman, with a surprised look on his face, remained in position at the door, until the defendant was escorted by the deputy sheriff out of the courtroom and back to Juvenile Detention.

Dan Singer turned, shook hands with Dr. Campbell, and spoke briefly about the next step. "You'll be granted permission to see Noah for fifteen minutes tomorrow morning," he said. "Following the sentencing, there will be no more contact." Dr. Campbell nodded.

"Noah will be immediately remanded to a facility assigned by the Judge," Singer said.

Rosie and Bucky walked out of the courtroom and headed for the elevator, intending to head home. Justin Overly was walking behind Ken Matthews and Nora Douglas. As they waited by the elevator, Rosie overheard Matthews talking to his sister-in-law.

That voice, she thought, *without a doubt, it's the one I heard on the phone.*

CHAPTER TWENTY-FIVE

The Sentencing - Part III

At home that evening, Rosie and Bucky were in front of the fireplace watching Luke and Jocko lying quietly side by side. They enjoyed the comfort of the room even when there were no warm flames crackling amongst the logs. Bucky had driven them home while Rosie had left her car parked at her building downtown.

"Want me to open a bottle of Shiraz?" Bucky offered.

"That would be nice," Rosie quickly accepted. She went over to the two animals and knelt to softly pet both dogs between their ears. They rolled over and she scratched their stomachs.

"Should I call Justin to say we're at home and the phone hasn't rung?"

At that precise moment, the phone came to life. Bucky quickly picked up the receiver.

"Is this the residence of Dr. Rosie Klein?"

"Who's calling, please?" Bucky responded.

"Hi Bucky, it's Wes Hill. I have some news that I think will interest Rosie."

"Just a second, Wes. I'll put her on."

Rosie took the receiver. "Hi Wes. What's up?"

"You'll never believe this but Ken Matthews was just arrested for tampering with your car in the LaSalle parking garage. The attendant, Geoff, saw him on a security screen and called Toledo police. Unbeknownst to you, he left the courtroom immediately after your testimony and hightailed it to your parking spot. He was flattening your tires. The police were checking your brake line, too. His sister-in-law drove herself up here from Columbus and doesn't seem to be involved."

"Wow. Now he can be charged with something. Prior to this, his calls weren't considered threatening, even though they were to me. Thanks Wes. I'll call Justin Overly and let him know. I wonder how he dodged Justin who was going to watch him until I called to say we were home. But we didn't receive any phone call from him either. Now, I owe you lunch. How about right after New Year's?"

Wes laughed. "Merry Christmas, Rosie. Be sure to read the Blade on Sunday."

Rosie dialed Justin's number and he answered on the second ring.

"Justin, there was no phone call when we got home and Wes Hill just called to say Ken Matthews was arrested for tampering with my car. Did he lose you?"

"My car was parked at a meter with a flat tire. I guess we underestimated Mr. Matthews.."

"Did you recognized him as the guy who wanted to solicit your services?"

"I did. You know what gave him away, Rosie? His

mustache and the big gold watch. He looked different when I first met him with his cowboy hat and boots on. But the watch was undeniable when he came to see me about following you," he said. "I guess he'll miss the sentencing hearing in the morning. Although he could be there if someone posts bail early enough for him. He probably called his sister-in-law and gave her some phony story since she's engaged in the outcome of this hearing. It's likely she's staying here in town."

"Well, thanks for calling, Justin. See you in the morning. I'd like to know what they do to someone charged with a misdemeanor."

The following morning, court convened as scheduled at ten o'clock.

"All rise," Bailiff Gorman called out as required. Judge Brown entered the courtroom from her chambers and assumed her position on the bench to begin the sentencing.

"Will the defendant please stand." It was more rhetorical than an actual question. Martha Dumphy stood to sign for Noah who also stood up, as did both of his attorneys.

"I've heard expert witness testimony from Dr. Rosie Klein, statements from the defendant, and from concerned witnesses, as well as the victim's family. Based upon all the information I have heard and reviewed, I am hereby ready to pronounce sentence.

"Noah Campbell, I sentence you to three to eleven years in prison on the count of first-degree manslaughter to be served for five years at Indian River until the age of twenty-one, followed by your remaining sentence at Allen-Oakwood

State Penitentiary. In addition, to be served consecutively, I sentence you to three years for burglary and four years for abduction of a minor child. The charges have been agreed to prior to this hearing. Court is adjourned."

With that, she hit her wooden gavel upon its wooden platform, stood, and left the courtroom.

Noah sat down and slumped in his chair. His attorneys told Martha Dumphy to sign that his time might be reduced with parole after good behavior. Noah saw his father approaching and stood quickly to embrace him. Standing by his side, a Sheriff's deputy waited a moment, then led him out a side door of the courtroom.

Noah looked back and noticed his mother wasn't there. What he didn't know was that she quickly slipped out of her seat in the back row and fled the moment the sentences were imposed.

EPILOGUE

Five years later:

Randy Evans was released from detention three years ago at age twenty-one, and has stayed in touch with Noah Campbell. He married his childhood sweetheart, Joanie, who stood by him all seven years he spent at Indian River for shooting his abusive father. Randy's career is going well and he and Joanie have started their family. They have two little boys, and one's middle name is Noah.

Noah Campbell has settled into his life-long cell at the "big joint." He's waiting to see Randy who plans to visit once Noah is allowed visitors after his first ninety days.

Mr. Campbell moved into a small cottage on Indian Lake to be close by his son and to visit on weekends. Retired from the University of Cincinnati, he now fishes from a small flat-bottom, sixteen-foot, fishing boat.

Mrs. Russell-Campbell is back from Portugal with her Ph.D. and a new career in Berkeley California. She is currently unmarried, but still keeps twenty-five hundred miles away from her son, Noah. Some things never change.

Chaplain Tom Beck stops by Noah's pod to assure him that he will spend time weekly if Noah wants to see him.

James Abraham, the boy from Zambia who knew American Sign Language, was sentenced to life without parole for his part in the murders of six people. He has now been in the penitentiary for eighteen years, where Noah is now, and knows the ropes.

Post Epilogue

Another Five Years Later in Noah's Own Words:

Noah Campbell - I've been in the "big house" five years already. I can't believe Randy Evens is back here, again, for good this time. Talk about screwing up!

Randy Evens, my role model, was living the life I could only have dreamed of having, but he caused his wife, Joanie's death, and basically made orphans of his sons, now being raised by his older brother, Roger, and his wife. I'm worried about him. He's obviously depressed. He started me journaling years ago, and now he doesn't pick up a pencil or a book, himself, ever.

When we aren't working, packaging the flags sown by women at Marysville Women's Reformatory, Randy just sits in his cell with his head hanging down or lays on his bed facing the wall. I'll try to connect him with **Chaplain Tom** and the medic, **Dr. Platt.** It may save his life. I know if it weren't for Chaplain Tom, I would not have believed God could love me, nor have a purpose for my life even in here. Through the Holy Spirt, I found the best way to serve God is to give hope to other incarcerated men, especially those serving life, as I am.

Miracles do happen. Maybe I will be paroled one day, and could become a prison chaplain. Hope is always the future. What else is there?

DISCUSSION QUESTIONS

How do you think Noah's father should have handled being a single parent of a young,special needs child?

What services should St. Rita's have provided to Noah after he was caught stealing?

Do you agree that grounding Noah in his room for a month was the most appropriate action? If not, what could the consequences have been?

If Noah had provided the names of the boys he was with on their "joy ride", what sentence should the Judge have imposed? Probation instead of incarceration?

What purpose did spending a year in the Juvenile Detention facility serve? Punishment? Rehabilitation?

The Principal of the Ohio School for The Deaf knew that Noah was entering their program after being released from Juvenile Detention. What assistance did they provide to help him adjust to the changes in his life? What suggestions do you have?

Did you guess who Dr. Rosie's mysterious caller was? What led you to this conclusion?

Do you believe that Noah did not plan to kill Misty Matthews? What do you think really happened?

Do you think that little Scottie Matthews said or did something to influence Noah to let him go, or was it Noah's plan all along?

As a Judge or Juror in Noah's trial, which witness' testimony would have influenced your opinion the most? Why?

Phyllis Kuehnl-Walters, Ph.D.

ACKNOWLEDGMENTS

I thank my husband, Dan, for his willingness to sacrifice time with me while I prioritize writing each day. He thought retirement would include nine holes of golf and lunch with his wife most days. Instead, I "re-fired" and turned my time and attention to producing true crime novels based on my life and career before him.

I also want to express appreciation to Paula Howard, my editor/publisher and good friend. She tells me the truth in love which serves to make me a better writer and storyteller.

I am grateful to Bob Hurley who used his talent to create the most meaningful cover jackets for all four of my books. Searching and sharing the photos he finds that coincide with the titles lends excitement to the sometimes boring tasks of a writer's life.

Lastly, I thank you, dear reader, for your support. I hope you enjoy this book as much as you enjoyed Dr. Rosie's first three adventures. Bucky guaranteed Rosie that her life with him would never be boring. I think he is absolutely right.

ACKNOWLEDGMENTS

ALSO BY PHYLLIS K. WALTERS

The Christmas Slayings

Wives Who Kill

Husbands Who Kill

Actual Reviews from Readers

THE CHRISTMAS SLAYINGS

". . . The reader is allowed into her casework and her romance with the handsome Bucky Walker. The romance on the side helps soften the reality of these cases.- *From Amazon- by J.J. Clarke, award-winning author of Dared to Run, a suspense thriller.*

WIVES WHO KILL

". . . This well-written novel brings to light the real and complex world of personal relationships where abusive partners or parents inflict damage upon those who they should be protecting. I look forward to reading Dr. Walters' next book."- *From Amazon- by Mel Harrison, author of three suspense novels*

HUSBANDS WHO KILL

"Phyllis K. Walters skillfully helps the reader understand what makes...perpetrators do what they do with a mix of compassion, while she blends in underlying humor to break up the seriousness of the subject. -*From Sally Galliers, beta reader*

THE CHRISTMAS SLAYINGS

Based on a True Story

PHYLLIS K. WALTERS

HUSBANDS
WHO
KILL
COUNTY
JAIL
Based on true stories
PHYLLIS K. WALTERS

ABOUT THE AUTHOR

Dr. Phyllis Kuehnl-Walters retired from a forty-year career as a psychologist in private practice and adjunct professor at the University of Dayton. She was affiliated with the Ohio University School of Osteopathic Medicine and served as a preceptor for medical students. Dr. Kuehnl-Walters specialized in forensic psychology and was appointed by many surrounding court jurisdictions to evaluate the mindsets of defendants charged with heinous crimes.

In her retirement, she has been "re-fired" as the author of four novels inspired by her role in determining the competency of defendants to stand trial, their legal sanity, or any mitigating factors for the purpose of sentencing.

Dr. Kuehnl-Walters is a member of the Florida Writers Association. Her previous novel, Wives Who Kill, was their May 2021 book of the month. She also maintains membership in the Writers League of The Villages, and the American Psychological Association (Emeritus). She enjoys speaking to book clubs and other organizations, including church groups, where she presents her three inspirational Christian books.

She and her husband have been on eight short-term mission trips sponsored by Washington Heights Baptist Church of Centerville Ohio and Fairway Christian Church of The Villages, Florida.

Dr. Kuehnl-Walters books are available on Amazon.com and at www.TheWritersMall.com/mysteries-thrillers . She can be reached at phylliswaltersauthor@gmail.com.

www.ingramcontent.com/pod-product-compliance
Lightning Source LLC
LaVergne TN
LVHW050640100826
845148LV00011B/1927

* 9 7 9 8 9 8 6 0 7 0 7 9 7 *